THE BHOPAL TRAGEDY

THE BHOPAL TRAGEDY

Language, Logic, and Politics in the Production of a Hazard

William Bogard

Westview Press
BOULDER, SAN FRANCISCO, & LONDON

Copyright © 1989 by Westview Press, Inc.

Published in 1989 in the United States of America by Westview Press, Inc., 5500 Central Avenue, Boulder, Colorado 80301, and in the United Kingdom by Westview Press, Inc., 13 Brunswick Centre, London WC1N 1AF, England

Library of Congress Cataloging-in-Publication Data
Bogard, William, 1950–
   The Bhopal tragedy: language, logic, and politics in the
production of a hazard/William Bogard.
      p.   cm.
   Bibliography: p.
   Includes index.
   ISBN 0-8133-7786-2
   1. Bhopal Union Carbide Plant Disaster, Bhopal, India, 1984.
   2. Pesticides industry—India—Bhopal—Accidents.   I. Title.
HD7269.C4515223   1989
363.17′9—dc20   89-9191
                                                                                  CIP

Printed and bound in the United States of America

The paper used in this publication meets the requirements of the American National Standard for Permanence of Paper for Printed Library Materials Z39.48-1984.

10   9   8   7   6   5   4   3   2   1

CONTENTS

TABLES AND FIGURES

PREFACE

Several years have elapsed since a gas leak at Union Carbide of India's facility in Bhopal marked the climax of a tragedy whose nightmare images will forever haunt the chemical industry. Forty years earlier, pictures of the complete devastation of a once vibrant Japanese city had much the same effect on a fledgling nuclear industry. Like the atomic explosion over Hiroshima, Bhopal continues to claim its victims long after the actual event. People still die from the lingering aftereffects of their initial exposure to the gas, and among survivors in the city a once unquestioning faith in the long-term economic and social benefits of chemical technologies has virtually disappeared.

How many have died? No one knows for certain. Official estimates from the Indian government place the figure at around 1,800, but unofficial tallies, which vary widely depending on what measures are used and whose interests are at stake, suggest anywhere from 2,000 to over 10,000 deaths. Personal injuries may have exceeded 300,000, and the impact on animal and plant life in the city was, by any measure, catastrophic. The loss in money terms is virtually incalculable. A decision regarding compensation for victims in the courts has taken nearly five years to achieve. All this while the victims of the tragedy continued to suffer. Government and corporate assistance has been painfully inadequate and marked by charges of stalling and corruption. Paradoxically, most of the human misery resulting from the tragedy came about in the name of the best intentions—to help the people of India overcome the most pressing problems of their economy, of overpopulation, and of a depleted and marginal agriculture.

Many different words have been used to describe what happened in Bhopal on the night of December 2, 1984: accident, disaster, catastrophe, crisis; but also sabotage, conspiracy, massacre, even experiment. While the latter four terms have infused the search for an impartial account of the gas leak with an air of polemic and political diatribe, the remaining terms—

though at first appearing to be more evenhanded and objective in char-
acterizing the event—are not for that any less evaluative.

Accident? Certainly. It caught virtually everyone by surprise, even though
some argued later that the type of accident Bhopal experienced was inevitable
sometime, somewhere, primarily due to the rapid global expansion of
complex chemical technologies. Disaster? Undoubtedly. Bhopal was the
worst industrial disaster in history, causing immeasurable losses to individuals,
families, and organizations. Catastrophe? Again, this is unquestionable. In
addition to the great harm done that horrible night in December, Bhopal
will be remembered as a massive testament to the fact that technological
disasters are not just historically fixed and geographically localized events;
rather, they generate perturbations of the social and ecological fabric that
are both long-term and highly unpredictable. Bhopal has indelibly altered
our consciousness of the interconnectedness of hazardous systems—both
natural and technological—and how the potential effects of hazards extend
broadly across human institutions and generations.

All these terms contain a partial element of truth, yet I have chosen
to describe the events leading to Bhopal as a tragedy. This is more than
mere verbal quibbling. How we label such events has political implications
for how we address and act upon a whole range of pressing questions:
Who, if anyone, was responsible for Bhopal? How should victims be
compensated for their losses? What, if anything, should be changed about
the way we adopt technical solutions to social problems in order to insure
that such a disaster will never again occur?

These questions suggest that Bhopal was more than a mere accident,
disaster, or catastrophe. Each of these descriptions minimizes, in its own
way, the problem of human agency and intention, and thus refuses to
address directly the issue of responsibility. In calling Bhopal a tragedy, we
are still permitted to say that intention and agency were involved in how
the event unfolded and that responsibility must ultimately rest with someone
or some group. But unlike saying that Bhopal was the deliberate result of
sabotage, a conspiracy, or some diabolical experiment involving human
guinea pigs—charges that are virtually impossible to prove in any case—
a tragedy, in contrast, emerges out of a complex of confused and misguided
intentions, many of which may be honorable in themselves but when forged
to the actual chain of events produce the worst possible outcome. Recent
criticisms of what happened in Bhopal that have sought to lay the blame
on some cabal must do so, despite a very legitimate sense of outrage, by
denying the fact that no one desired such an outcome. If we are to place

blame, we must have a way of doing so that takes into account that most persons directly involved in Union Carbide's operations in Bhopal genuinely believed that they were doing the right thing and that they were helping a beleaguered nation faced with great and seemingly insurmountable problems.

So there are no villains in this book, although it is highly critical of the roles played by the Union Carbide corporation, the professional class of risk analysts and hazards experts, and the Indian government itself. It is critical, despite these actors' best intentions, of what can only be called their unquestioning faith in technical (and thereby hazardous) solutions to tremendous human problems, and their too-ready willingness to turn a blind eye to the hazard of chemical manufacturing and label it a calculated risk taken in the pursuit of humanitarian ideals. Indeed, ignorance of the effects of their actions does not excuse the *principal* players, but takes them to task precisely for their unwitting participation in the succession of events.

This amounts to saying that a double sense of the term *tragedy* is applicable to Bhopal, one that parallels the distinction between principal players and victims. For victims of the gas leak, Bhopal was a true tragedy. There was a genuine inevitability in the catastrophic loss of life and livelihood to persons that were denied reliable information regarding chemical hazards and how to defend themselves when exposed to such hazards. For the principal players, on the other hand—Union Carbide, the Indian government, and their technical/organizational supports—the tragedy was a false one. There was no inevitability in their actions or the consequences that followed from them. Other decisions regarding the implementation of hazardous technologies could have been made, and better choices were within reach. If responsibility is the question, the answer is clear. Whether or not a conspiracy will ever come to light (or even if the disaster was the result of industrial sabotage, as some representatives of the corporation have claimed), Union Carbide itself was responsible, the government of India was responsible, a technocratic class that predictably elects profitable, low-cost, high-tech answers for human misery was responsible. Theirs is a responsibility grounded on intentional ignorance, deliberate omission, and misguided optimism.

My original purpose in writing this book was to offer a critical theory of hazards, which the Bhopal tragedy would serve to highlight. Because my training is in sociology, my primary interest in investigating the tragedy was its relevance to issues in the areas of social organization and social conflict. I quickly realized, however, that if my goal was to understand and evaluate the general global development of hazardous systems that provided the overall context for Bhopal, sociological models alone were inadequate. The roots of the Bhopal tragedy extend to the political economy of development in the Third World, to the logic of technical choice, and finally, to the language we use to conceptualize, detect, and weigh hazards in our environment. Specifically, I became convinced that the true origins of the Bhopal tragedy lay in how political power and scientific expertise combined to change the public's perception of what was hazardous and, more significantly, what was safe. The stage for Bhopal was set in the first instance not by any specific technical failure (although this was certainly a factor) and not by the rather obvious motives for profit from the sale of pesticides on the part of Union Carbide (although this, too, was certainly relevant and important) but by the way in which the hazard in Bhopal was defined and finally glossed over and how these definitions mirrored a generalized practice of minimizing the global hazards of chemical production by labeling them "acceptable risks," i.e., by using the most sophisticated technocratic and scientific arguments available to generate an ultimately *false* image of safety and benefit. The gas leak in Bhopal that December night in 1984 was so deadly only because its victims felt no hazard, experienced no prior threat. Only the manipulation of the language of hazards, deliberate or otherwise, could have produced such misguided complacency. Bhopal was indeed an accident insofar as it was a complete surprise, but the stage was carefully prepared beforehand by expert proclamations of safety to insure that it was only an accident waiting to happen.

What follows is not a theory in any strict sense. I do not have any illusion of having finally explained how tragedies like Bhopal happen, at least not in the sense of forwarding claims that could be empirically verified. In any case, theory alone does little good for the victims of the disaster. What I have called theory in the body of the text is perhaps better characterized as a set of critical reflections, a provisional and abstract model of the innumerable factors that would make the account of Bhopal provocative and extreme, that would provoke debate and, ultimately, redefine our unreflective and culturally embedded acceptance of technocratic definitions of a hazard.

More persons contributed thoughtful comments to this book than I can mention in a brief introduction. In particular, I would like to thank Drs. Dennis Mileti and Charles Perrow for their comments and criticisms of an earlier draft. I doubt that I have addressed all of their concerns adequately, but their impact is here even if I have been unduly stubborn about clinging to my own ideas. They share no responsibility if it fails to convince. I also extend my thanks to Shirley Muse and Whitman College for help in preparing the final draft of the manuscript.

Ultimately, I have been guided only by the sense of outrage that disasters like Bhopal are allowed to happen at all and by the belief that intellectuals themselves, despite disclaimers, have a real hand in how such tragedies unfold. How do we balance the risks and benefits of our increasingly hazardous technologies? How can we insure that there will be no more Bhopals? We must constantly be aware that merely posing this question in the accepted language of hazards may not turn out to suggest the outlines of a possible answer, but may unexpectedly involve us in aggravating the problem.

William Bogard

1

THE BHOPAL TRAGEDY

Levels of Explanation

If the prolonged atmosphere of contention following major technological disasters[1] in this century tells us anything, it is that a definitive account of the Bhopal tragedy—one that would be completely satisfactory to everyone—is unlikely. The interrelated *system* of hazards—global, regional, and local—that sets the stage for massive catastrophes like Bhopal is always too complex and permeated with uncertainties. This system virtually defies any specification of causal mechanisms that would claim to be exhaustive. This certainly doesn't imply that an explanation for what happened in Bhopal is impossible–the present book does indeed aim at the form of a possible explanation. Nor does it mean, as one well-known social scientist suggests, that the ultimate cause of all technological disasters is just this very *complexity* of hazardous systems (Perrow 1984, p. 7). Rather, it means that as new information about the Bhopal tragedy is uncovered, and constructing credible answers becomes the goal of institutionalized forms of discourse, the specification of possible causes will necessarily bear the marks of conflicting interests—of scientists, the press, corporate managers and employees, politicians, lawyers, judges, and victims.

In this book, I shall not be concerned so much with exposing the "real" or "objective" causes of the Bhopal disaster as with the strategies that different interested parties have used to conduct their search for causal hypotheses, how they have utilized scientific-causal language or politico-economic rationalizations to articulate their own interests *vis-à-vis* hazardous production technologies and social ecologies, and how their accounts and actions over time have transformed the public perception and evaluation of hazardous systems. From these accounts I hope to construct a general model of how hazards like those that existed in Bhopal come to be defined and symbolically manipulated—primarily through the institutionalized use of expert knowledge and political persuasion—and what the potential effects of this process are in terms of vulnerability or actual harm to persons.

In short, I am shifting the level of analysis from the conventional specification of material causes for the disaster to the level of the social and political interpretation of hazards, how certain hazards are selected from the range of environmental threats to become "problems," and, ultimately, how their public detection is constrained. I must note that my intention in stating the problem in this way is not to conduct what has come to be known as a subjective risk assessment (SRA). Since this form of analysis bases its conclusions on data which reflect culturally predefined categories of risk and safety, it routinely sets to one side the question of its own effective role in the public process of hazard identification and evaluation. Without attempting to deny the merit of SRA, I am far more interested in its cultural and political functions within hazardous systems than as a tool for my own analysis of the Bhopal incident.

Of course, a strategy focusing exclusively on the interpretation of hazards cannot tell the whole story. Given the complexity of the issues raised by the disaster, I cannot avoid bringing in other relevant considerations—it would be absurd to claim that all or even most of the factors contributing to the disaster were merely social or interpretive in nature. An understanding of the Bhopal tragedy can only result from the application of multiple perspectives. In the following pages, I will have the occasion to examine the internal logic of technical production, the global economy of hazards involved in technology transfers to the Third World—particularly the transfer of chemical technologies—the public resources available to cope with environmental dangers, constraints on scientific prediction, and a variety of other concerns. Each of these are important and relevant considerations in an explanation for the tragic waste of human life in Bhopal. Nevertheless, from the *sociological and political* perspective I am adopting here, I will continue to insist that *any* explanation, even those emphasizing the role of global economy and technical rationality, will inevitably be the outcome of a symbolically negotiated struggle attempting to fix responsibility for the event. With this in mind, we can turn now to the examination of some current hypotheses for the catastrophe.

Technical and Human Failures

Literally thousands of pages have been written on the Bhopal tragedy from a variety of critical perspectives (cf. Kurzman, 1987; Shrivastava

1987; Banarjee, 1986; de Grazia, 1985; Everest, 1985). It is not surprising, therefore, that current hypotheses for the tragedy in Bhopal are located on a variety of system levels. They have ranged from technical and human failures inside the plant (Bidwai 1985b), to corporate negligence (Bandyopadhyay 1985), to regulatory failures on the part of the U.S. and Indian governments (Ramaseshan 1985a), to failures in general agriculture and technology transfer policies (Mojumder 1985).

Many times an accident like the one at Union Carbide's facility in Bhopal can be traced to faults, errors and omissions within the component technology of the facility or to mistakes in operating this technology. With regard to technical and human failures inside the plant, an analysis conducted by the *New York Times* (January 28–February 3, 1985) shortly after the accident revealed a number of interrelated problems. When employees initially discovered a methyl isocyanate (MIC) leak at 11:30 p.m. on December 2nd, 1984, their shift supervisor, believing it was most likely a water leak, postponed an investigation until after his work break. Several months before the accident, a refrigeration unit designed to inhibit dangerous chemical reactions in the storage tanks at the Union Carbide facility was shut down, ostensibly for cost-cutting reasons. Other critical mechanical safety devices were also inoperative or failed at the time of the leak. These included a mechanical vent scrubber designed to detoxify escaping gas with caustic soda, a network of water spouts intended to neutralize MIC vapor by transforming it into relatively safe organic compounds, and a 30 meter high flare tower located a short distance from the MIC unit designed to burn toxic gases high in the air, rendering them harmless. A spare tank built to hold an accidental release of MIC was not empty at the time of the leak and could not be used to prevent the gas from escaping.

According to the MIC supervisor on duty at the time of the accident, some of the instruments for detecting pressure and temperature levels of the chemicals produced at the plant prior to the accident were unreliable, and there was a conspicuous lack of redundancy measures—computer backups. automatic shutoffs and alarm systems—that might have detected and stopped the gas leak before it spread beyond the confines of the plant (*New York Times*, 28 January, 1985).

One hypothesis for the accident suggests that pipes at the MIC production unit were cleaned by an improperly trained technician. This may have introduced a small amount of water into the storage tank containing the bulk of the MIC, causing an unstable chemical reaction and buildup in pressure. In weeks following the disaster, the Carbide corporation claimed that the amount of water introduced into the storage tank may actually have been quite large, and their investigation of the way in which pipes had been reconnected was used as evidence for the hypothesis that the disaster was not the result of a simple employee mistake, but rather indicated the possibility of deliberate sabotage. Still another hypothesis suggested the possibility of slow chemical reactions of MIC with the stainless steel walls of the storage tank itself (Bidwai 1985a, p. 58). Each of these hypotheses were extended and refined as the technical details of the plant's operation came increasingly into public view during the endless rounds of litigation which followed the accident (cf. Kurzman 1987).

Corporate Negligence

No sooner had technical and human failures at the Bhopal facility been postulated than countercharges of hazards operating at a more general level arose—pointing to negligence on the part of the Union Carbide Corporation and its corporate subsidiary Union Carbide of India, Ltd. (UCIL), which had the responsibility for taking care of the day-to-day operations of the facility. People asked why there were no effective public warnings of the hazard. The alarm that eventually did sound on the night of the accident was identical or similar to those sounded for other purposes, including practice drills, about 30 times in a typical week (*New York Times* 1985a). No safety brochures or other information on hazards had been distributed in the "bastis"—the poor squatter's slums surrounding the plant. Finally, there was no public education program about what to do in case of an emergency (*New York Times* 1985a). For these and other reasons, Carbide's charge of industrial sabotage did little to minimize the public anger directed toward the company. Many persons who identified with the victims of the disaster were not sympathetic to Carbide's allegations, seeing in the sabotage charge only another corporate attempt to cover its own systematic negligence and misinformation campaign about the hazards that existed at the Bhopal facility.

The U.S. based transnational company owned a 51% share of its Indian operations and was responsible for the design of the plant and the education of its operatives (*New York Times* 1985a). The board of directors of UCIL included members of the parent company. Before the accident, sales of UCIL's pesticide products had been declining in India, and profits failed to live up to projected figures made at the time the company applied for and received the go ahead to expand its facilities to produce MIC in 1973 (Bidwai 1985c, p. 71). From the time of its startup in 1977, the MIC unit in Bhopal never manufactured more than half of its capacity for pesticides that was allowed by its agreement with the Indian government (Sharma and Singh 1985, p. 82), and it has been charged that this lack of profitability, stemming from a depressed market for its products, was the prime reason for severe and ultimately unjustifiable cutbacks in employment, training, and safety at the facility (Ramaseshan 1985b, p. 41).

Regulatory Failures

Charges of corporate irresponsibility in the pursuit of profit have produced their own countercharges and moved the chain of causal hypotheses for the Bhopal tragedy to a third level—regulatory failures on the part of the Indian government and its relations to Union Carbide and its Indian affiliate (*New York Times* 1985d). The Bhopal plant experienced six accidents between 1981 and 1984, at least three of which involved MIC or phosgene, a highly poisonous gas used in World War I and a component in the manufacture of MIC. The accidents were generally small scale—one worker was killed in 1981—but official inquiries required by law were often shelved or tended to minimize the government's or the company's role. A 1982 safety audit by an inspection team from the parent company turned up a number of problems at the plant, including several of the human and technical failures noted above, but failed to share some of this crucial information with its subsidiary (Bowonder et al. 1985, p. 8; Lueck 1985).

The Indian government did very little to address the problem of large numbers of people settling in proximity to the Bhopal plant. Indian law generally prohibits the construction and operation of highly hazardous production facilities in populated areas (Ramaseshan 1985a, p. 98). During the 1970s, several attempts were made to get the Union Carbide plant relocated to a safer area, but failed as a result of strong opposition from the government of Madhya Pradesh, the state where Bhopal is located. The government's argument against relocating the facility was that it had originally been set up on "barren land" and that it could not control the subsequent mushrooming of bastis near it. But even in 1969, when the initial license for the facility was applied for, there were at least 50 bungalows around the site as well as the Institute of Education and a colony set up by the Bhopal Development Authority (Ramaseshan 1985a, p. 95). The Bhopal railway was only 3 km. from the plant and the area around the station contained a sizeable population that worked in the local textile mill. In 1984, squatters' rights were given to those in the burgeoning settlements surrounding the plant, setting the stage for the high casualty rates following the accident (Ramaseshan 1985b, p. 37).

Relations between Union Carbide and the governor of Madyha Pradesh were cordial—as some charged, perhaps too cordial. The company provided a lavish guest house in Bhopal for the governor and visiting dignitaries along with special wards in the local hospital for their medical care (Ramaseshan 1985b, p. 38). Officials tended to be very lax in their enforcement of regulations when labor related problems arose at the plant and did little when these problems led to the dismissal of labor union representatives. Within the government itself at least one individual—an administrator with the Bhopal Municipal Corporation—who tried to bring up questions of vulnerability to those inside and in immediate proximity to the plant was forced to resign and take up a new position outside Madhya Pradesh (Bhandari 1985a, p. 104). After the actual accident, there was little evidence of concern, other than the usual statements of regret and promises of an investigation, from local and national government officials, many of whom declined even to visit the site of the tragedy (Ramaseshan (1985b, p. 45).

Agricultural Production and Technology Transfer

The conspicuous hesitation to act on the part of Union Carbide and the Indian government—whether intentional or otherwise—both before and after the December 2nd disaster raises considerable questions with regard to state and corporate interests in agricultural production and technology transfers to the Third World. According to World Health Organization statistics, almost half a million people are poisoned each year by pesticides. Of this number, the United Nations Environment Programme has estimated that as many as 22,000 die, and that this figure is growing at a rate of 5% each year (United Nations Environment Program 1979). This alarming rise in the number of pesticide-related deaths has been linked to the rapidly increasing number of manufactured toxic chemicals and their world-wide export to poorer nations without first adequately determining their toxic properties. At the present time, there may be nearly 40,000 different untested chemicals in use, and it may take up to 80 years before their toxic properties are fully determined (Gupta 1985, p. 151; Norris 1982, p. 5). Many of these chemicals have been banned or strictly regulated in Western nations, but their export continues unabated to the Third World in a practice known as "dumping" (Rele 1985, pp. 156–157). In 1981, the United States lifted a ban installed by former President

Jimmy Carter on the export of these untested chemicals. They now find their way into the hands of Third World farmers, who may mix them with other chemicals, apply unsafe amounts to their plants, or store them near their own food sources. In an accident like Bhopal, they find their way into the homes of the industrial slums that inevitably spring up around manufacturing centers in the overcrowded cities of the Third World (*New York Times* 1985e).

Pesticide production in India grew side by side with the advances of the so-called Green Revolution—the introduction of new seed grain varieties designed to increase food supplies and induce a measure of economic and political stability in that nation (Farmer 1977, p. 1). These new strains required a wholesale change in the technological and social infrastructure to support them—changes in water and land management, farmer organization, etc.—and prompted the demand for increased production and consumption of pesticides. In India alone, pesticide consumption increased from 25,000 tons in 1970 to almost 96,000 tons in 1984 (Mojumder 1985, p. 146). No one knows the long term effects of such increased consumption on health or the natural environment. The spreading effects of the use of pesticides may be pernicious, accumulating in the oceans, in the bodies of plants, animals, and humans, and eventually even winding up back on the kitchen tables of those nations who have banned their domestic use (Carson 1962; Norris 1982, Chapter 2).

The manufacture of MIC-based pesticides was not the only available solution for poor agricultural production in India and other parts of the Third World. Natural methods of pest control, judicious farming practices and genetic controls might all have proven safer and just as effective (Mojumder 1985, p. 146). There was nonetheless considerable pressure from transnational corporations like Union Carbide to adopt quick Western technological fixes for these agricultural problems (*New York Times* 1985e). The lack of strictly enforced regulations, combined with a large supply of cheap labor in the Third World, are strong incentives for these corporations to ignore costly and untried alternatives to the production of synthetic organic pesticides such as those formed with MIC.

Of course, transnational corporations typically reject the attribution of such motives. These enterprises understand their own actions as providing a needed *service* in the agriculturally impoverished regions of the Third World. Chemical producers, usually in collaboration with exporting and host governments, see an accident like Bhopal as the unfortunate price to be paid for two important and necessary *mitigations*—protecting the world's hungry against the ravages of potential famine, and thereby effectively insuring a degree of economic and political stability for the nations of the Third World.

Levels of Explanation in the Hazards System

Each of these hypotheses invokes the causal operation of a hazardous process that could explain the disaster. The hypotheses vary in their scope and level of generality; they appeal to hazards that are quite specific and localized, such as the potential failure of component safeguards, but also to hazards that are generated at the level of global socio-economic policies.

In no case is an ultimate, definitive, or totally satisfactory causal explanation of the tragedy in Bhopal likely to be found. Instead, one is confronted with complex ecological, social, and technological systems of interacting hazards on the one hand, and a similarly complex *discursive* network of conflicting and contradictory interpretations of this system on the other—a discursive network that articulates the rationalizations and problematizations of corporate executives, technocrats, union officials and workers, the press, the State, and, of course, the actual victims of the tragedy. These groups rarely perceived the hazards system surrounding Bhopal in the same way.

Before we examine the various levels of explanation for the tragedy more closely in the following pages, it is important to note that the same operations could be defined as hazardous by one interested party yet seen as perfectly safe and necessary by another. Such attributions are common where normative questions arise concerning the potential effects of implementing particular technologies. Where Union Carbide's managers and state officials justified MIC technology by appealing to the safety of the Bhopal facility, its efficient organization and mechanical operation (even, remarkably, after the accident), journalists and others were just as quick, at least in retrospect, to point out the hazards. The incommensurate values attributed to Carbide's operations in Bhopal suggest an underlying *discursive logic* involved in the definition and perception of hazards. I will attempt to specify in later chapters how this logic both enabled and constrained the recognition and detection of the hazards at the Bhopal facility, in the populated regions surrounding the production site, and in top-level policy decisions affecting chemical exports to the Third World.

Leaving aside the details of this argument until later, my general thesis is that the transfer of chemical technologies and products to Third World nations from the West is also the discomforting story of an inherent tension in the interpretation of hazardous processes. The more such technologies are successfully defined and categorized as *mitigations* (defenses against agricultural and economic deficits, famine, or internal political dissent, for example), the less likely it is that an exposed public is able to perceive and evaluate the *hazardous features* of these technologies for itself. Now if persons in positions of authority claim that something is safe, the public is certainly free to believe them or not. All too often, however, the general public is required by constraints on their time and energy to trust "expert knowledge" in these matters. This form of trust—the belief that expert knowledge will be employed in the public interest and for its protection— is also the transfer of public responsibility to detect and evaluate hazards to the state, safety planners, risk analysts, and corporate elites. If hazards thereby go undetected, and if as an unfortunate consequence of this the public feels safe and secure, it virtually eliminates any prior capacity on the part of the public to plan for its safety and respond effectively to an emergency. The hazard remains there in some "objective" sense but, in effect, disappears from public view. The tragic result can be increasing hazardousness and vulnerability—paradoxically, the safer the public feels, the higher the level of danger.

From the more detailed account of the Bhopal disaster to follow, we shall see that the detection of hazards was blocked at virtually every level of the hazards system for an exposed public. An overriding and ultimately unjustified feeling of safety colored the decisions of Union Carbide and the Madhya Pradesh government. It was the poor, however, who knew the least about what was happening in and around the Bhopal site at the time of the accident. It was the poor who believed most that the hazards system associated with the production of chemicals was both contained and beneficial to them.

Limiting the Detection of Hazards by Processes of Definition

We know from accounts in the Indian and American media that serious conflicts of interpretation arose regarding the causes of the tragedy between Carbide, the Indian government, and victims. On the other hand, conflicts regarding the *potential* for catastrophe in Bhopal were quite rare—and less publicized—in the period before December 2, 1984. Here I will provisionally introduce the concept of "definitional strategies" to refer to discursive means for selecting, identifying, evaluating, and justifying exposure to hazards (risks/potentials for harm).[2] These strategies include, but are not limited to, rules for conducting cost-benefit analyses, establishing hazardous thresholds, marking the extension of causal hazards chains, and for deciding when not to decide to address a potentially hazardous situation (non-decisions). I will examine each strategy more formally in following chapters. For now, I am concerned only with selecting some representative examples from the Bhopal case that indicate the usefulness of such an analysis in a preliminary way.

Even though their intention is to make hazards more visible, definitional strategies can hide as much as they reveal. Although ideally it is a public discourse, defining hazards today has become the practical task of an elite social class comprised of corporate executives, scientists, government officials, and safety planners. This is an admittedly heterogeneous class, but one for which the general term "technocratic" is, for my purposes, entirely appropriate. In Bhopal, I will argue, the discourse on hazards actually had the function of limiting residents' chances for detecting danger. More specifically, the technocratic appropriation of this discourse had the un-intended effect of redirecting an exposed and vulnerable public's attention away from the primary hazard in Bhopal—that is, the actual production of toxic and lethal chemicals—through claims that overemphasized or exaggerated the safety and necessity of this production.

In searching various accounts of the situation in Bhopal for definitional strategies that could have limited the public detection of hazards, I was specifically interested in language that suggested that potential hazards were actually not hazards at all but had primarily beneficial or mitigative effects. Both the *New York Times* analysis cited above and various Indian newspaper sources contained a variety of texts, some critical and some not, indicating that many persons, professional and non-professional, believed "adequate precautions" had been taken at the Carbide facility, that safety was for the most part unaffected by a potentially hazardous process, or that certain problematic practices constituted an "acceptable" or "necessary" risk (cf. *New York Times* 1985c). Here we turn to the first of these strategies—cost-benefit analysis—as it applies to the case at hand.

Cost-Benefit Analysis

As noted, staff, training and equipment levels at the Bhopal facility had been severely cut back prior to the accident. Since 1983, the number of operatives working in the MIC unit had been reduced from 12 to 6 and the overall number of blue collar workers concerned with the details of the plant's operation had been reduced from 850 to 642 (*New York Times* 1985a; Bidwai 1985c, p. 73). The refrigeration unit that had been designed to keep MIC at a safe storage temperature had been shut down in an effort to save electricity and freon for use elsewhere in the plant. V. P. Gokhale, the chief operating officer of UCIL, termed these cost-cutting measures as simply an effort to "reduce avoidable and wasteful expenditures" that did not dramatically affect overall safety (Diamond 1985a, pg. A6).

Although some of the workers at the Bhopal plant had complained about these cost-cutting measures, the U.S. parent company said it did not think that reduced spending had resulted in the malfunction of key safety equipment (Lueck 1985, p. A7; Ramaseshan 1985b, p. 41). The company maintained only that "cost reduction is a continual objective of managers throughout the world, and UCIL, like other subsidiaries, has used *operations improvement* programs," a curious twist of language (Leuck 1985, p. A7; emphasis mine). Union Carbide's U.S. managers further claimed that responsibility for establishing training, manpower, and safety requirements rested solely in the hands of its subsidiary, despite the fact that it maintained a controlling interest in the Bhopal operation. It cited UCIL's decisions as simply ways for "improving and making more efficient" the plant's production (*New York Times* 1985b).

The move to economize the Bhopal plant's operations can be traced to a dull and sagging market for Union Carbide's pesticide products in the late 1970s. An alpha-naphthol plant originally scheduled to have been completed as part of phase I of the pesticides project was abandoned in 1982 and the money invested written off by the company (Bidwai 1985c, p. 70). Maintenance procedures were severely curtailed and the shift relieving system was suspended. This meant that if no replacement turned up at the end of a shift the following shift went unmanned. Workers were routinely denied access to gloves or gas masks as a result of cost cutting measures, a policy that, combined with job losses and high employee turnover, was in part responsible for the demoralization of many workers (Bidwai 1985c, pp. 71–72; Ramaseshan 1985b, p. 41; Diamond 1985a). Equipment checks and testing of samples of materials also appear to have become less frequent after 1982 (Bidwai 1985c, p. 71).

Despite the cutbacks, UCIL's brochures continued to depict an optimistic picture for the plant's future (Sharma and Singh 1985, p. 82). They made no mention of the facility's economic problems, but rather continued to link the overall safety of the production process with the country's need for a solution to the problem of pest infestation (Sharma and Singh 1985).

The hazards of MIC possibly leaking into the atmosphere were never mentioned in these brochures, effectively eliminating one possible source for residents around the facility to detect and possibly devise coping strategies for the hazard.

Setting Thresholds

In the Bhopal accident, a number of thresholds established for the production of and exposure to methyl isocyanate were surpassed. The threshold limit value (TLV) for exposure to MIC is set at .02 parts per million (PPM), which is an extremely high level of toxicity (Kumar and Mukerjee 1985, p. 131). Because of this extreme toxicity, MIC has been the subject of few biochemical studies and little is known about possible treatment for exposure, which produces severe complications. Several days after the accident, it was still uncertain whether the effects being observed from the gas leak were due to MIC or phosgene, another extreme toxicant used in MIC's production. Treatment of the exposed population was thus limited to symptoms because no scientific agreement could be reached on what might constitute an appropriate antidote (Fera 1985, p. 51).

Threshold limits for exposure to MIC were inadequately understood by workers, residents, and scientists alike and this tended to minimize the perception of the hazard. Since MIC itself was poorly researched in the scientific literature, little was known about its effects on specific organs of the body or its long range effects on the environment (Menon 1985, p. 135). At the Bhopal plant itself, in the absence of reliable detection mechanisms to accurately gauge threshold levels, plant operatives were told to be aware of eye irritation as the first sign of exposure. This led to the widespread belief (re: misunderstanding) that MIC was only an eye irritant and not fatal (*New York Times* 1985c). For one whole week following the disaster, the Indian government failed to assure the citizens of Bhopal on whether the air they were breathing or the water they were drinking was safe. At a press conference on December 6th, the chief minister of Madyha Pradesh declared that the air was totally safe. Despite this pronouncement, air samples had not yet left Bhopal to be tested in Delhi (Ramaseshan 1985b, p. 46). Bhopal itself lacked the equipment for such tests. The minister also declared water safe to drink but nevertheless cautioned residents to boil their water before drinking it, raising considerable doubts about the reliabiity of sample tests (Ramaseshan 1985b, p. 46). Some held that threshold value levels established for MIC were only a corporate mechanism designed to get workers and residents to accept the hazardous conditions at the plant (Menon 1985, p. 137). Many workers believed the .02 ppm TLV to mean nothing more than "reasonable freedom from irritation, narcosis, nuisance or other forms of stress" (Menon 1985, p. 137). Setting thresholds also had an impact on the actual production of MIC and the safety mechanisms designed to prevent an actual leak. The head of India's Council of Scientific and Industrial Research, Dr. Varadarajan, noted that routine tests at the MIC unit in Bhopal failed to adequately measure the reactivity of MIC with chlorine ions present in the production process. Such a reaction, as we have seen, was one hypothesis for the critical buildup in temperature and pressure that preceded the leak (Diamond 1985c). The tests were assumed to accurately assess when certain thresholds had been surpassed. Varadarajan was also troubled by the absence of basic research on the stability of MIC, particularly when it was stored in such large quantities—15,000 gallon tanks—as was the case in Bhopal.

Plant procedures at Bhopal specified that the refrigeration unit must be operating whenever there is MIC in the system. The Bhopal operating manual says that the chemical must be maintained at a temperature no higher than five degrees Celsius. It specifies that a high temperature alarm is to sound if the MIC reaches 11 degrees Celsius. Because the refrigeration unit had been turned off, the chemical was usually stored at nearly 20 degrees Celsius. In response to this, plant officials had readjusted the threshold of the alarm from 11 to 20 degrees Celsius, thus limiting the early detection that would have been possible when the temperatures started to rise (Diamond 1985a).

Various other safety mechanisms at the plant also had design thresholds that were inadequate to counter the magnitude of the leak on December 2nd. The vent scrubber, had it worked at all, was designed to neutralize only small quantities of gas at fairly low pressures and temperatures. The pressure of the escaping gas during the accident, however, exceeded the scrubber's design by nearly 2-1/2 times, while the temperature of the gas was at least 80 degrees Celsius more than the scrubber could handle (Bidwai 1985b, p. 65). Similarly, the flare tower intended to burn off released vapor was totally inadequate to deal with the estimated 40 tons of MIC that escaped in the accident (Bidwai 1985b, p. 65).

Despite inadequate thresholds in testing and design, UCIL and Union Carbide persisted in their presentation of the plant as a "model" facility in the safe production of pesticides, and representatives often boasted of the plant's complex technology (Sharma and Singh 1985, p. 82). Just prior to the accident in Bhopal, Union Carbide's safety and health survey of its

MIC Unit II plant in West Virginia cited a number of concerns about reduced surveillance and monitoring of hazards that were quite similar to problems the Bhopal plant was experiencing. The parent company, however, failed to notify its subsidiary of these concerns, mainly on the grounds that the two plants cooling systems for MIC were substantially different (Bowonder et al. 1985, p. 8). Equally problematic was the parent company's overriding of an alleged UCIL protest against the installation of the extremely large storage tanks at Bhopal noted above. MIC sat in storage in these tanks at least three months prior to the accident, a length of time that almost invites the type of chemical reactions hypothesized to have caused the buildup in temperature and pressure (Bowonder et al. 1985, p. 8).

Limiting Causal Chains

"Limiting causal chains" refers to a strategy designed to constrain the discussion of causes for an accident to a predetermined set of potential mitigative failures. With regard to Bhopal, this strategy is exemplified in retrospective accounts which stress that *no further steps could have been taken by way of policy or design to halt the onset of the disaster.* J. Mukund, Carbide's works manager at the time of the accident, expressed precisely just how the idea of limited causal chains affects the perception of a hazard. On being informed of the accident, his immediate reply was one of disbelief: "The gas leak just can't be from my plant. The plant is shut down. Our technology just can't go wrong, we just can't have such leaks" (quoted in Bidwai 1985d, p. 29).

Such disbelief was also widespread among almost everyone directly associated with the production of MIC prior to the event and literally prevented plant operatives, health workers, corporate managers and government regulators from seeing beyond the existing system of mitigations designed to forestall the accident. Workers said it was common practice to leave MIC in the spare tank at the plant, although standard operating procedures required that it be empty. The plant had experienced such problems with hazard detection instruments in the past to the extent that even when they worked reliably and recorded "real" changes—one gauge in the MIC unit actually recorded a fivefold rise in the storage tank's pressure—these changes were often ignored (Diamond 1985a). While several investigators from Union Carbide traced the cause of the accident to a human error--water entering the MIC storage tank from an improperly cleaned pipe at the plant—they tended to downplay design or cost cutting factors (Bidwai 1985b).

It is usually standard practice in hazardous facilities to include a large amount of redundancy in the safety systems along the production line (cf. Perrow 1984, pp. 94–96). The Bhopal plant, however, had low rates of redundancy, or none at all, in some of its crucial components (Bidwai 1985b, p. 66). This was particularly true with the control and instrumentation system installed in the factory. There were few automatic alarms or interlock systems that might have warned operators of abnormal conditions in critical locations or at important junctions. In many chemical plants, pneumatically operated pressure gauges have electrical or electronic backups. On tanks and reactors holding dangerous chemicals, for instance, there may be two or three pressure and temperature gauges placed in different positions, although for "normal" purposes one may be enough. In contrast to this, the Bhopal system, despite company disclaimers that it was one of the most technologically sophisticated in the world, had antiquated and mainly pneumatic indicators and gauges. There was only one pressure level indicator gauge and one temperature gauge on each of the three MIC storage tanks, although common practice might have indicated two or three on such large vessels (Bidwai 1985b, p. 67). In at least 15 different vital positions in various parts of the MIC complex there were only indicators of temperature and flows where there should have been perhaps recorders as well, which maintain a permanent record of all critical parameters. Backups were also absent in the interlock system at the plant and in the interconnections in the plant's control room. The vent scrubber, which failed to work in any case, had no automatic activation system (Bidwai 1985b, p. 67).

It is not immediately clear, of course, that the existence of backup systems would have lowered the level of hazardousness and vulnerability in a facility like Bhopal. As Perrow (1984) has rightly noted, complex control systems introduce a variety of uncertainties into production processes and may interact to generate unpredictable failures. The reliance on complex backups may also give rise to unwarranted feelings of security that divert attention away from the most immediate form of the hazard, viz., the production of hazardous chemicals itself. One writer in the Indian press suggested that the Union Carbide management employed the chemical company's history of relatively safe production to divert attention to system types of failure rather than to questions concerning the need for chemical pesticides in the first place (Mojumder 1985, p. 146). In this sense, i.e., in terms of management's interests, the causal chain of the hazard did not extend beyond the factory walls at the Bhopal plant.

Even after the accident at Bhopal, a great deal of effort was extended to shift perceptions that the gas coming from the plant was not MIC at all. Doctors treating affected residents initially thought the disaster was due to phosgene, a component in MIC's manufacture. What the phosgene hypothesis immediately achieved was to confuse doctors to the extent that no attempt was made to find or administer or even consider the question of an antidote seriously (Fera 1985, p. 52). Phosgene's effects were much better known than MIC, and this knowledge reinforced the tendency to discount recommendations that patients be treated for MIC exposure (Fera 1985, p. 52). Patients and residents themselves had trouble believing such serious consequences could stem from a leak at the plant. Neither the highly toxic aspects of MIC nor instructions about what to do in the event of an accident were made available to them by UCIL, Union Carbide, or the Indian government. For the poor in the bastis surrounding the Bhopal plant, the extended chain of causes was not even remotely visible.

Non-decisions

A non-decision can be defined simply as an act of omission, although in the present context it refers to the extrusion of information that might be used in making a technical choice. Both before and during the accident at Bhopal, persons in key positions were alerted to potential dangers from a number of sources but "decided" to do nothing, either believing risks were too low to justify action or consciously limiting access to the decision-making process regarding these risks. In either case, the structure of non-decisions limited the public ability to detect the hazard, and management capacity to provide a timely warning to the people of Bhopal. The lack of decision-making was widespread and involved plant managers, the media, corporate spokespersons, and the Indian government. Accounts suggest that no individual or organization wished to take responsibility for the accident despite the fact that, in hindsight, a number of actions could have been taken to mitigate the timing and the extent of the disaster (cf. Ramaseshan 1985a, pp. 95–101).

Employees seldom worried about internal leaks at the plant, in part because they were routine occurrences (Diamond 1985a). The problems were either fixed without further examination or ignored. After the accident, when calls were made to the plant to find out what had happened, inquirers were repeatedly told that everything was under control. UCIL managers did not sound the warning siren until after 2 a.m., over two hours after the leak was discovered, nor did they make an effort to notify the police or civil administration in Bhopal. Police queries to the plant about the nature of the accident generally went unheeded between 1 and 2 a.m. (Bidwai 1985d, p. 29).

Information regarding the health hazards involved in the production of MIC at the Bhopal plant prior to the accident was difficult to gather. The Carbide company conducted routine health checks of employees but would not make the information gathered from these tests available to workers or to the unions that represented them even after repeated requests (Ramaseshan 1985b, p. 38). The labor unions were also reportedly denied access to the Indian press in their attempts to publicize what they saw as repeated safety and health violations at the Bhopal plant. Labor union leaders maintained they were consistently harassed or silenced when they tried to bring violations to the attention of the public (Ramaseshan 1985b, p. 38). The only media outlet that appeared to be an exception to an alleged policy of ignoring union charges was a small circulation weekly in Bhopal, *Rabat*.

When the media finally did acknowledge the problems at the Bhopal plant, it was only subsequent to the actual disaster. Investigating journalists who rushed to the scene following the tragedy were met, however, with the evasion of corporate executives and government officials who refused to speculate publicly on the causes of the accident or address the problem of responsibility. The chief operating officer of UCIL declined comment on alleged violations in safety equipment at the plant, in particular the shutdown of the refrigeration unit at the MIC facility (Diamond 1985a). Spokespersons for the U.S. parent company in Danbury, Connecticut similarly maintained they had only incomplete information on the safety procedures of the Bhopal plant and declined any comment other than to stress they had no grounds to believe such an accident could occur. Despite repeated requests for interviews, the Carbide company declined to make its chairman, Warren M. Anderson, its vice-president for health and safety, Jackson B. Browning, or any of its scientific experts available, citing incomplete information, the desire to avoid speculation, and ongoing investigations as the reasons for their refusal (*New York Times* 1985a; Lueck 1985).

Perhaps the most important non-decisions in the Bhopal story were, however, prior to the event and revolved around the various omissions of the Indian government itself. From the time the license for the pesticide plant was granted in 1969 by the Indian Congress government, officials sat tight on a large amount of data assessing the hazards involved in MIC production. This appeared to be the case despite several accidents at the plant, indications by the Pollution Control Board that environmental standards surrounding the plant were being exceeded, and the protests of the town planning administrator. The latter was forced to resign from his position while attempting to convince government administrators of the need to relocate the factory away from populated areas (Bhandari 1985, p. 104).

The government appeared to be indifferent to the growth of slums, smaller factories, and residential colonies in proximity to the plant, despite regulations prohibiting such developments (Ramaseshan 1985a, p. 98). Rather than relocate either the plant or the residents (many of whom because of their work would have been severely disadvantaged by moving), the government decided to make no decision in the matter until it ultimately granted squatters' rights to the poor in the bastis next to the plant. The concerns of plant operatives themselves went unnoticed. Labor union letters to the state and central governments, demanding that the Bhopal facility be categorized as a heavy chemicals industry and thereby be brought under the review of the more stringent Indian laws applicable to this form of industry, have to date gone unacknowledged (Ramaseshan 1985b, p. 40).

The Indian government possessed much of the necessary information to evaluate the potential hazards of the Bhopal plant. This is fairly clear from the fact that the State Electricity Board was in possession of all the required documents that were handed over to it each time the Carbide company applied for increased power. The Industries Department of the state government was probably also given the same, if not more detailed, data (Ramaseshan 1985a, p. 97). The possession of this information is difficult to reconcile with the Madyha Pradesh government's claim to have had inadequate information on the Bhopal plant at the time of the accident. With the hazards rating of the Union Carbide plant spelled out so specifically for these two agencies, it remains a mystery why the government did not probe more deeply into some of the problems the plant experienced before the actual accident.

Definitional Strategies and Their Implications
for Detecting Hazards at Bhopal

Each of the definitional strategies examined above—cost-benefit analysis, setting thresholds, limiting causal chains, and non-decision—acted to rearrange the possibilities for detecting the chemical hazards that existed in

Bhopal prior to and during the accident of December 2, 1984. Despite the problems the plant experienced in its day to day operations and the extremely hazardous nature of the materials produced there, the overall perception of its operations remained one of relative safety. At least this was true up until the actual disaster. This was possible because a perception of safety was the effect of the defining strategies themselves. Paradoxically, each of the above strategies was itself in essence a *mitigation*, i.e., a *tool* for enhancing safety. Cost-benefit decisions could thus be seen as an integral feature of an "operations improvement program." The dangers involved in dramatically cutting back on plant personnel or the refusal to upgrade safety equipment were presented as smaller risks than those that would be involved in closing down the plant itself due to its unprofitability. A thorough cost-benefit analysis assured a relatively unconcerned public that no unnecessary risks were left unaccounted for in the final tabulation. It was in this way that hazards resulting from cutbacks in operations could be discursively transformed into their exact opposites. Plant operations could now be seen as "streamlined" or more efficient rather than just barely meeting safety requirements.

The same process can be seen at work in the setting of thresholds for exposure to MIC. Despite its extreme toxicity and the limited scientific tests conducted on this chemical, the very *idea* of a threshold redirects the emphasis away from criticism of chemical production *per se* to a justification for believing that certain levels of exposure are tolerable or an acceptable risk. As long as tolerance levels are set and enforced, it is presumed that handling the chemical is safe. The fact that these levels themselves are subject to many uncertainties is masked by the appearance of an objective procedure for establishing these levels. The overall effect is to allow continuation of the production of the chemical because it is now perceived to be safe.

A pattern thus begins to emerge for how social defining strategies operated to constrain possibilities for detecting hazards in Bhopal. Both limiting causal chains and non-decisions had the function of preventing broader issues regarding the production of hazardous chemicals from coming to the foreground. In simply noting the relatively minor nature of chemical accidents at the Bhopal plant prior to December 2nd, Union Carbide and the Indian government possessed a powerful argument for their respective refusals to install backup safety equipment or to move the plant away from populated areas. The extrapolation from the past safety record of the plant, which in reality was not all that good but was presented as such, was in essence an *excuse or alibi* for failing to deal squarely with the potential,

however small, of a catastrophic accident. The assurance that past performance is an adequate guide in the assessment of hazards is itself an
incentive for maintaining the status quo. In offering such an assurance,
however, concerns about the general hazardousness of chemical production
as a technology that may be best dispensed with altogether never reach
the political agenda. Chemical production has, as a result, been made
"safe."

Uncertainty and Counterfinality

Prior to an accident, detecting hazards is an imperfect process at best
and involves a logic of uncertain outcomes. Tragedies like Bhopal are
literally the result of not recognizing dangers that, so to speak, stare people
in the face. This section only begins to scratch the surface of the myriad
gaps in knowledge that beset the manufacture of hazardous chemicals in
Bhopal and how they interacted to produce unintended—or "counterfinal"—consequences for the residents of that city.[3]

As endemic features of complex productive systems, uncertainty and
counterfinality force us to examine relationships that extend beyond the
gates of the Union Carbide facility or the city limits of Bhopal, and which
have implications for hazardousness and vulnerability throughout India and
the Third World. Here we must begin to consider the production of
hazardous chemicals within the framework of a *general system* of hazards
and mitigation comprised of a variety of subsystem levels—technological,
ecological, and socio-political. In doing so, I do not mean to generalize
the case of Bhopal indiscriminately to a larger context. I only wish to
suggest that an understanding of this larger context is necessary to make
sense of the specific events that culminated in the Bhopal tragedy. It is
for this reason that I shall insist that the *global system of chemical production*
must stand as a necessary reference point for any analysis of the disaster.[4]

Uncertainty

Many uncertainties came to the public's attention only in the wake of
the Bhopal accident, and they crosscut a number of analytically distinct
levels in the production process. Uncertainties about MIC's toxic effects
abounded in its research and development phases. At the Carbide facility,
they were generated by unreliable instrumentation, untested safety equipment and procedures, and by the often ambiguous roles of the plant's

maintenance and supervisory personnel. In the background there were always global uncertainties about the long-term impact of pesticides on the natural environment.

In the community, widespread ignorance of the plant's operations seriously compromised the ability of residents to respond effectively to the release of gas. In view of the paucity of information actually circulated to residents concerning the toxicity of MIC, very few of them knew that a simple damp cloth placed over the face could have saved them from lethal exposure at the time of the leak (Bowonder et al. 1985, p. 32; Diamond 1985a). In retrospect, it is incredible that so many people could have been caught by surprise. Even in spite of the fact that MIC itself was not a thoroughly researched product, warnings from the parent company to its subsidiary were usually quite explicit about the potential dangers of the chemical, and one must look to factors that complement uncertainty to explain why persons generally believed that exposure to MIC would not affect their health. The politics of detection plays a large role here. The relentless promotion by Carbide, UCIL, and the Indian government of the Bhopal facility as a symbol of state-of-the-art technology in the service of progress undoubtedly led to a false association in some peoples minds of the level of technical sophistication at the plant with the actual safety of the product (*New York Times* 1985d). Besides, how could a chemical that is used on agricultural products be lethal? Such illusions might account for at least some of the lax behavior exhibited by all parties prior to the release of gas.

Despite the common belief that personal safety was not unduly threatened before the accident, this belief was quickly shattered when persons started to experience the adverse effects of exposure firsthand. Residents suddenly had to confront, on the most harsh terms, all the uncertainties and potential problems that had been glossed over for years by the Carbide company in its brochures and public announcements. The routine mix of indifference and trust that characterized Bhopal's attitude to the company gave way to a paralyzing atmosphere of indecision when the feeling of safety literally vanished in the terrible reality of the accident.

Uncertainty was the rule of the day in Bhopal. Rather than heightening the awareness that something might go wrong, it appeared to block it. Lack of adequate information about MIC delayed the use of warning sirens during the leak (Diamond 1985a). It fostered an apathetic attitude among UCIL's employees to routine mishaps at the plant and to the value of emergency drills. It promoted the government's minimal enforcement of regulations for hazardous substances. Finally, uncertainty was a factor in the inability of Bhopal doctors to decide on the proper method of treatment for injuries (Bidwai 1985d, p. 30). Not more than a handful of doctors believed that MIC exposure was the explanation for numerous deaths fully a week after the event. Whether this would have made a difference anyway is rendered irrelevant by the fact that medical science knows of no antidote for MIC poisoning (Menon 1985, p. 135).

Despite the uncertainties involved in MIC production, community preparedness, medical treatment, and the like, uncertainty itself appears never to have been a practical criterion for decisions about the design or warning procedures of the Bhopal facility. This is suggested both by the general disregard for publicly advertising worst-case accident scenarios and in the numerous holes in the fail-safe system monitoring the production line itself (Bidwai 1985b). It is not possible to say that devaluing the role of uncertainty as a decision criterion was a deliberate policy of either Union Carbide, UCIL, or the Indian government to promote the appearance of safety. Still, at the time of the accident, Union Carbide was allegedly involved in research and production of chemical warfare technology at its research center in Bhopal (Press Trust of India 1985, pp. 140–142; Delhi Science Forum 1985). It is possible that its interests in keeping such sensitive operations secret led the company to minimize public information about uncertainties at both facilities. In any case, it appears that both real gaps in information and the general disregard of uncertainty as a decision criterion led to a failure to detect the hazards at the Bhopal plant on the part of all parties.

Counterfinality

The uncertainties surrounding the Bhopal accident combined in diverse ways to produce (or have the potential to produce) counterfinal or unintended outcomes. Again, this is apparent at all system levels directly or indirectly affected by the production process.

Practice alarms at the plant, as noted above, sounded so often that an actual alert, which ironically was delayed during the accident, could not be distinguished from tests (*New York Times* 1985d; *New York Times* 1985a). When the danger became known, many employees of the plant ran from the contaminated areas, totally ignoring the buses that sat idle on the grounds ready to evacuate nearby residents (*New York Times* 1985a).

Counterfinality, uncertainty, and non-decisions combined in universally unquestioned assumptions about the adequacy of safeguards at the plant.

No one seemed to seriously believe that all of the crucial safety mechanisms at the facility could fail simultaneously. Hence, no plans were made for the contingency that the vent scrubber, the flare tower, the water spouts, the refrigeration unit, and various monitoring instruments could fail to work at the same time (Reinhold 1985).

Counterfinality was also the outcome of massive demographic changes spurred by an industrialization campaign in which Carbide and other transnational corporations would have a significant role. Slums surrounding UCIL's plant—like J. P. Nagar (where 300 people died)—were the product of economic and social forces that have altered the face of urban India over the last two decades. Impoverished villagers have migrated by the thousands into cities like Bhopal seeking work at the new factories (Bowonder et al. 1985, p. 7; *New York Times* 1985e). Since UCIL obtained the license from the Madyha Pradesh government to produce MIC in 1969, the population of Bhopal has more than doubled, from 350,000 to over 800,000 (Bowonder et al. 1985, p. 7). Finding no housing, no public assistance, and very little work, migrants have been forced to live illegally on whatever unoccupied land they could find. Increasingly, local governments have yielded to pressure to allow them to stay. This (non)decision, combined with the city's unwillingness to relocate the facility, probably contributed to the belief that the plant was safe enough where it was. What is certain is that the high population density of the area surrounding the plant directly contributed to the large loss of life and injuries.

At the most general level where counterfinality combines with uncertainty, one must place the Bhopal tragedy in the context of speculation regarding the long-term effects of pesticide production and consumption on health and the natural environment. In India, the consumption of pesticides has risen at a staggering rate, multiplying by almost 50 times in actual tonnage since the early 1950s (Mojumder 1985, p. 146; also Gupta 1985, p. 151, who cites a somewhat more modest figure of 36 times). Despite regulations, there is evidence of a widespread and gradual increase in pesticide poisonings among citizens. Of all the developing nations, India accounts for at least one third of the world's cases of such poisonings (Norris 1982, p. 26). Tragically, all this has happened and been justified in the name of an ultimate *mitigation*, viz., the protection and enhancement of the domestic food supply.

Exaggeration of the benefits of pesticide production for the Indian economy has systematically diverted attention away from its potentially negative long-term consequences for the natural environment. When pesticides are released into the environment they enter meteorological and biological cycles that distribute them widely around the world in concentrated form, much in the manner of radioactive fallout. Hydro-environments seem to be particularly affected (Kumar and Mukergee 1985, p. 133). Ironically, countries whose regulations prohibit the use of certain pesticides often find them back on their own tables in the form of food exports from developing countries. Despite these counterfinal outcomes, unregulated and untested chemicals exported to the Third World are increasing dramatically and alarmingly (Norris 1982, p. 20).

Some Initial Reflections Regarding Uncertainty and Counterfinality

In Bhopal, a number of actions that originally appeared rational and well-intentioned produced collectively irrational outcomes. Tests of warning sirens at the plant desensitized residents to their function in the event of an emergency. The forward-looking actions of the Indian government in licensing the plant drew thousands of squatters to areas directly outside the plant's walls. At higher levels, the short-term benefits of reducing agricultural pests seemed increasingly in conflict with the cost of polluting, perhaps irreversibly, the natural environment. The list goes on.

I cannot overemphasize that the accident came as a complete surprise to almost everyone. This was true not only for the residents of Bhopal, but also for Union Carbide's own scientists and risk assessors (Bowonder et al. 1985, p. 6). The paucity of worst-case scenarios, despite the fact that this is a routine consideration in the implementation of most hazardous technologies, is extremely troubling in view of Carbide's optimistic public presentation of the Bhopal facility (Bidwai 1985b). The absence of such scenarios had to be an important factor in contributing to the lack of hazards detection in Bhopal. This is evident in typical reactions during the accident itself. The belief that such a catastrophe could not happen with such modern technology, that so many safety systems could not fail simultaneously, that the Bhopal plant was a "model" facility, etc., directed necessary attention away from the overall production process and its possible worst consequences and fostered a general atmosphere of safety (*New York Times* 1985c).

The atmosphere of safety that surrounded the Bhopal facility was part and parcel of the almost unquestioning faith in Western technologies as the cure-all for some of the most pressing problems of Third World development—agricultural deficits, economic stagnation, and rapid population growth. This faith paralleled the phenomenal rise in the growth of the chemical industry in the West over the past several decades. How this rise linked up with global economic pressures to export huge quantities of chemicals to the Third World, and how these pressures further complicated the detection of hazards in developing countries, is the subject of the following concluding remarks.

Global Economic Pressures in the Production of Pesticides

Economic pressures for producing pesticides in India were as significant and varied as the uncertainties surrounding the project. Particularly important to consider are the relations between UCIL's need to operate its plant profitably and how this need may have compromised the enforcement of local environmental regulations designed to insure safety at the plant. These two factors were also associated with the political need to solve the problem of India's marginal and erratic food supply, and particularly with the problem of how to rapidly secure technology transfers from the West for the Green Revolution (Farmer 1977). Predictably, global economic pressures tended to exaggerate the mitigative potential of pesticide use for the Third World economy and divert attention from its hazards. Increasingly, pesticides came to be seen as an integral component in peripheral states development (Mojumder 1985).

Before proceeding to the actual details of how global economic factors may have limited hazard detection in Bhopal, it is necessary to place this process in context. The following brief account provides an overview of the history of the chemical industry and its links to the problem of Third World export policies. Again, such a strategy is not specifically intended to make inferences from the Bhopal tragedy to similar situations that may arise in developing nations. The intent is rather to formulate the general socioeconomic conditions within which the Bhopal event occurred, i.e., with reference to the general theoretical logic of hazards which follows in the next two chapters.

The Economic History of the Chemical Industry

International trade in chemicals grew at an exponential rate during the 1970s, from an estimated worth of $22 billion in 1970 to $96 billion in 1978 (U.N. Conference on Trade and Development 1981). During this same period, the value of exported chemicals to developing countries in the Third World increased from $5 billion to $24 billion (a figure which includes not only pesticides, but pharmaceutical and industrial chemicals). As noted above, many of these chemicals have been "dumped" on the Third World, a practice in which core manufacturing corporations sell or dispose of products banned or unapproved in the home country (Rele 1985, p. 155; also Norris 1982, p. 2).

The chemical industry itself is fairly young, not much over 150 years old. In 1828, the German chemist Fredrich Wöhler synthesized the first organic compound, urea, an excretory product of many animal species. This discovery introduced a whole new era of industrial development in the West, and today literally tens of thousands of manufactured chemical substances are commercially available throughout the world.

Wöhler's work changed fundamental thought about the nature of chemical reactions and spawned an explosion of further research. By the 1920s, the chemical industry had become an important factor in the growth of many industrial nations. The introduction of new fertilizers, pesticides, and insecticides, all of which depended on the rapid growth in research on chemical substances, rose at a steady rate during the first four decades of the 20th century. After 1940, however, the rate of growth has been tremendous (Fig. 1.1).

As World War II ended, the use of chemical compounds in agriculture expanded rapidly. During the 1960s and 1970s, large scale Western agricultural technologies were introduced to many farming societies in the Third World, spurred on by the Green Revolution, which boosted crop yields by introducing capital-intensive and chemical-dependent practices such as mechanical farming and improved varieties of grain. The latter were especially dependent upon the widespread and consistent use of fertilizers and pesticides (Farmer 1977, Chap. 1; Super 1980, p. 17; Chambers and Farmer 1977). From 1974 to 1978, Third World imports of pesticides increased from $641 million to almost $1 billion (Food and Agriculture Organization 1979). Thirty-eight percent of the international trade in pesticides came from the Third World (Food and Agriculture Organization 1979).

The U.S. has been increasingly reliant on the trade in pesticides, and from 1976 to 1978 almost doubled its export sales from $625 million to over $1 billion. Although U.S. production rose by 50% during the 1970s, export to foreign countries increased by 200% (U.S. Department of Agriculture 1979). Of the increased exports in pesticides, 30% were unregistered, i.e., unapproved by the Environmental Protection Agency,

FIGURE 1.1 U.S. Chemical Production Increase Between 1900 and 1980
Reprinted from Ruth Norris (ed.), Pills, Pesticides and Profits: The International Trade in Toxic Substances. 1982, p. 5. Croton-on-Hudson, New York: North River Press. Used by Permission.

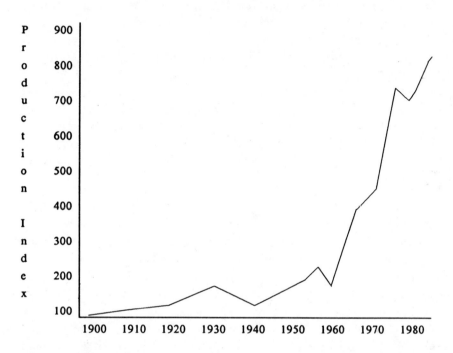

for use in the United States. Many of these unregistered pesticides were formerly registered but subsequently banned when their dangers became known. Significantly, these bans did not extend to the Third World. U.S. corporations continue to manufacture pesticide products for the Third World that are considered unsafe at home, taking advantage of the lack of international regulations in the trade in chemicals and the pressing need for increasing food supplies in developing countries. These latter countries themselves, in their efforts to modernize and achieve a relative degree of self-sufficiency, have been noticeably lax in implementing strict regulations that would limit the import of dangerous chemicals (Rele 1985, p. 157). Increasingly, hazardous production facilities that have come under stricter regulation in the U.S. have themselves been imported wholesale into these countries.

The U.S., however, is neither the only nor the largest exporter of pesticides to the Third World. Germany is first (25%), followed by the

U.S. (20%), the United Kingdom (15%), Switzerland (15%), France (13%), and Japan (5%) (U.N. Yearbook International Trade Statistics 1979). Interestingly, German production of the pesticide MIC was based upon a chemical process considered safer and less toxic than the one developed by the U.S. and subsequently exported to Bhopal. Why the U.S. process was chosen remains a mystery, although one can speculate that the prestige of the United States in the world market and domestic pressure for Bhopal to have a state of the art chemical facility which would provide much needed employment in the city were factors. Union Carbide itself, as I have indicated, may also have had other interests in the research and development of chemical weapons technologies in Bhopal (Press Trust of India 1985, p. 140). The official reasons for actual siting of the plant may never come to light, but there is enough information to raise disturbing questions about the political and economic motives behind the decision to build the facility.

Union Carbide's Operations in Bhopal

In spite of denials, it appears the Union Carbide company in Danbury, Connecticut had substantial authority over its affiliate (Bhandary 1985, pp. 102–106). As noted above, the parent company had representatives on UCIL's board of directors and maintained a controlling (51%) share in the Indian company (New York Times 1985a). Many of the day to day details, such as staffing and maintenance, were left to Indian officials, but every major decision, such as the annual budget, had to be cleared with the American headquarters, and directives were often issued from the U.S. (New York Times 1985a). The parent company also had the right to intervene in day-to-day operations at the plant if it thought safety was being compromised. Even so, crucial safety violation information turned up by parent company inspectors was not always turned over to UCIL managers (Bowonder et al. 1985, p. 8).

Other problems indicating discrepancies in Carbide's public and private postures emerged. These concerned the relatively low output of the Bhopal plant. In 1983, pesticide production was only 31% of the licensed capacity of the facility. Ostensibly this was because of the declining profit picture for pesticide production during the 1970s and early 1980s (Sharma and Singh 1985, pp. 82–83). This raised some disturbing questions. It was suggested that some of the plant's output may have been used for experiments at the Carbide Research Center in Bhopal for processes for which UCIL was not authorized. Sharma and Singh (p. 83) note also that underproduction is often a technique used by corporations to control supply and maintain profit levels. In light of the parent corporation's public stance, which was to withhold comment on all aspects of operations until all information on the disaster had been gathered and analyzed, such charges are difficult if not impossible to verify (cf. *New York Times* 1985a).

As the plant lost money, many of its skilled workers, sensing an uncertain future, left for other jobs and were either not replaced or had non-skilled workers substituted for them (Bidwai 1985c, p. 70). Despite the minimal training of many of these new workers in how to handle non-routine emergencies at the plant, no consideration was seriously given to the idea of shutting the facility down (Diamond 1985c). The idea of spending money now on training to avoid future problems later was an alien concept to UCIL's directors, who tended to make decisions solely on considerations of profitability (Ramaseshan 1985b, pp. 37–41). Training levels suffered while the perception of danger usually went unchanged (*New York Times* 1985d).

Several months before the accident, the Town Planning department of the Madhya Pradesh government listed 18 local industries as "obnoxious" and held that these industries had to be subject to continuous assessment for their impact on the environment. The list made no mention, however, of the pesticides industry despite the fact that tests conducted by the Madhya Pradesh Control Board indicated several violations of environmental quality standards at the Bhopal plant (Ramaseshan 1985b, p. 37). Even though it is true that fairly comprehensive environmental laws existed on the books at the time of the accident, a substantial amount of evidence suggests that Indian officials and planners often looked the other way when alleged environmental and safety violations at the Bhopal facility were brought up. The phosgene leak in 1981 that killed one worker in the plant did generate an official inquiry, but the report gathered dust in the Madhya Pradesh labor department until after the accident in 1984 (Bowonder et al. 1985, p. 8; also cf. Rele 1985, p. 157; Goyal 1985, p. 163; Gaya 1985, pp. 168–173; *New York Times* 1985d).

We have seen that in India the pesticides industry has grown concomitantly with the development of the Green Revolution (cf. Farmer 1977; Prasad 1983; Norris 1982). The introduction of new seed varieties more often than not carried with it the necessity for increased pesticide applications. The need for such pesticides as insurance for the continued success of the Green Revolution was not, however, accompanied by an infrastructure of regulation and enforcement to guard against the negative short and long-term effects on health and the natural environment of the burgeoning industry during the 1960s and 1970s (Rele 1985, p. 157).

Critics of pesticide use in poor Third World countries have charged that manufacturers in core industrialized nations have taken advantage of food supply problems in states such as India and their lower enforcement standards for regulating hazardous industries in order to market products that are either banned or severely restricted at home (Gupta 1985, p. 153). India's often unreflective need for Western technology combined with lax regulation and large supplies of cheap labor provided an ideal context for marketing and testing chemical pesticides that were not acceptable in core countries. In Bhopal, the Union Carbide Corporation was one of six multinational companies that were allowed by India's Department of Science and Technology to conduct controversial chemical research without clearance from higher governmental screening agencies (Press Trust of India 1985, p. 142).

Despite the critical hindsight offered by the tragedy in Bhopal, prior to the accident Union Carbide and the Madhya Pradesh government worked hand in hand to insure the success and profitability of the company and thus indirectly to benefit the Indian drive for modernization. The Indian government offered the site on which Union Carbide constructed its plant for an annual rent of less than $40 per acre (Bowonder et al. 1985, p. 7). Alternatives to MIC production that involved the use of less toxic intermediaries were not given serious consideration, even though such alternatives were clearly available from similar MIC facilities operating in Europe at the time (Ramaseshan 1985a).

Some Conclusions Regarding Economic Global Pressure

Prior to the accident, companies such as Union Carbide were highly regarded by government planners and technicians for their assistance in helping India to achieve economic self-sufficiency and political stability. During this time Carbide was generally perceived to be a model company (Diamond 1985a; Bowonder et al. 1985, p. 7; New York Times 1985e). Even after the accident, however, global pressures continued to operate against the expulsion of Union Carbide from India. Despite official statements that the facility would be nationalized or shut down completely, many believe that the plant will reopen in the near future (Diamond 1985c; New York Times 1985d). Jobs are needed in this region where unemployment is high and there is no welfare system. It is argued that companies such as Union Carbide provide the country with the technology, skills, capital and equipment that might otherwise take years to develop indigenously. Such arguments are clearly opposed to those whose initial premise is that the Third World has become the dumping ground for the hazardous technologies of multinational corporations (Rele 1985). Such charges and countercharges abound today in the Indian press. At issue, however, is not the evidence or lack of evidence to corroborate these charges, although the data itself is convincing. The issue is rather how the current polemic, backed by global economic demands and pressures—for adequate food, self-sufficiency, political stability, and environmental integrity—has itself altered the perception of hazardous technologies.

Before the accident, arguments stressing the mitigative aspects of hazardous technology transfers apparently held sway since few parties clearly perceived the dangers. The average Bhopal citizen's trust in Western solutions for their most pressing problems blinded many of them to the inherent problems of rapid industrialization. The outcome was increased hazardousness and vulnerability, particularly for the poor of Bhopal who had no reason to disbelieve either the statements emanating from the Carbide corporation or its own government.

Conclusion

In this chapter, I have traced some of the system mechanisms that limited the public detection of the hazards associated with the production of pesticides in Bhopal. In the following pages I shall tie some of these observations to reflections about increasing hazardousness and the vulnerability of the poor in Bhopal and, more cautiously, to what this process may mean for the introduction of hazardous technologies in general. I have specifically avoided the search for an ultimate cause for the accident itself, relying instead upon a description of a complex series of defining processes, uncertainties and counterfinalities, and global pressures that, working together, ultimately resulted in the tragedy.

There are limits to the generalizations that can be drawn from an analysis of the Bhopal tragedy, but these limits must be relaxed given that the accident that occurred there was so terrible in its scope. If an accident like Bhopal is not to repeat itself elsewhere, certainly some general lessons can be drawn from the Bhopal experience that would apply to other areas of the Third World. In any case, the Bhopal accident cannot be adequately understood except in the light of a general framework in which related concerns regarding the safety of hazardous technologies can be analyzed.

The Bhopal tragedy may not be representative of all industrial accidents in the twentieth century, but it exemplifies the impact of uncertainty, counterfinality, catastrophic potential, and dependence on Western technology transfers for the solution of agricultural, political and economic problems common to all Third World countries. For these reasons we cannot wait for more tragedies of this sort to occur in order to make some limited theoretical generalizations. This will be my aim in the following two chapters.

In the last chapter I will make several recommendations, based on the experience in Bhopal, for the evaluation of hazardous chemicals. These recommendations are derived from questions concerning the dependency on chemical pesticide technologies in the Third World, the uncertainties associated with their use, and the catastrophic potential they embody when placed in the context of complex technological systems. These recommendations are themselves flawed and incomplete, for they must be balanced against the real needs for food and the elimination of poverty and dependency in the Third World. No solution can be totally satisfactory, for all solutions to the problem of hazardousness and vulnerability themselves function as mitigations and have a potential for failure. Such solutions must therefore be put forward with caution. The intent of these recommendations is to make detectable once again those hazards that have been glossed over by pressing economic and social needs in the nations of the periphery, needs that are themselves the products of global pressures for modernization. If the Bhopal tragedy has anything to teach, it is the necessity to concentrate not only on specific mitigative techniques for saving lives and protecting the health of particular residents in particular locations from the dangers associated with hazardous production facilities. It is the necessity for questioning the need for such facilities in the first place and the global system that demands their construction.

Notes

1. Although I shall continue at times to use the conventional distinction between "technological" and "natural" disasters, it will become increasingly clear that I do not take such distinctions too seriously. The present work intends to develop a general interpretation of hazards in which historical data from both so-called natural and technological events is relevant. In any case, when social and cultural factors are taken into account in the analysis of these events, the line between "acts of man" and "acts of God" loses much of its force. Disasters—and the hazards which create their potential—occur at a complex interface of technological,

natural, and social fields, and no study is complete without an explication of the typical and atypical relations between each of these fields. On this point, see Wijkman and Timberlake (1984), *Natural Disasters: Acts of God or Acts of Man*. Earthscan.

2. I chose to use the term "definitional strategy" rather than "analysis of risk" to avoid both the mathematical connotations of the latter concept and its association with an overly narrow group of practitioners. It is the *cultural politics* of risk assessment that I am interested in here. Controlling the definition of risk—and safety—is, from this perspective, a process of argumentation, persuasion, and strategy in which a number of competing groups in society participate.

3. I shall discuss the notion of counterfinality more extensively in subsequent chapters. In theoretical terms, counterfinality refers to outcomes of action that, while rational in the individual case, are irrational for the collective. Many types of hazardous processes exhibit counterfinal features—they embody routines that are often undertaken for the best motives but, when followed by everyone, can have catastrophic consequences.

4. A global perspective enables specific links to be drawn between and within subsystems in terms of their interactive contribution to the production of hazards— between, e.g., agricultural practices, eco-environments, social organizations, technology, cultural values, language, etc. The disaster in Bhopal, as many authors have noted (cf. Shrivastava 1987; Kurzman 1987), reintroduced disturbing questions about modernization, urbanization, industrialization, and development in both core and peripheral nations—questions which only a global framework is capable of addressing adequately.

2

BHOPAL AND THE CRITICAL
THEORY OF HAZARDS

Hazards and Disasters

In the city of Bhopal reminders of the nightmare on December 2, 1984 are a common sight. Many of those who survived that night are the victims of the debilitating aftereffects of chemical poisoning. Most will never fully recover. They are the ones who have permanently lost both their health and their meager economic livelihoods to the disaster.[1] State assistance to the survivors at best has been painfully slow and confused in a welter of bureaucratic and legal tangles. And many have suffered the loss of close friends and family.

To all this one must add the misfortune that the tragedy itself has quickly disappeared from the public conscience, not only in the West but to a lesser extent in much of the Third World as well. Litigation between Union Carbide, victims of the accident, and the Indian government continues, and the disaster has produced some reforms in the chemical industry (in the United States, for example, a national emergency hotline has recently been established). But Bhopal has long since lost its force as a "headline" event, and the most pressing questions posed by the disaster are still unanswered. What are the prospects for similar disasters in the future? Are such disasters today more likely—a result, perhaps, of the increasing hazardousness of modern industrial cultures? Which groups are most vulnerable to these hazards, and which are most likely to be harmed if an accident of this type recurs? Because of the tremendous uncertainties and partisan claims that inevitably accompany the attempt to answer these types of questions, no explanation can be assumed to satisfy everyone. But surely, we simply compound the tragedy in failing to ask them.

Even more vexing are questions of a philosophical and theoretical nature: what precisely *is* a "hazard" and what do we mean when we speak of "hazardousness." Similarly, what kind of state or process is signified by the term "vulnerability"? In both the social sciences and in geology, where these terms first gained academic currency a short 40 years ago, "hazardousness" and "vulnerability" are essentially contested concepts.[2] The contemporary practice in the new subdisciplines known collectively under the rubric of "hazards research" has been to define these terms operationally, that is to say, as quantifiable phenomena expressed in levels of risk, and to pass over for the most part their political or moral implications. But in view of the relative newness of this research programme, there is comparatively little quantitative research, and far less theory of critical import, bearing directly on the questions of hazardousness and vulnerability to hazards.[3] This lack is all the more pronounced when these questions take on a global dimension, i.e., when they enter the international debate surrounding modernization and development, the role of technology in the deterioration of the natural environment, hazards arising from geometric population increases, urban concentration around industrial sites, terrorism, nuclear strategy, and so on. Worse, the bulk of the findings we do possess are derived from simple extrapolations of information gathered on past *disasters* and only marginally adds to our theoretical understanding of *hazards*, which are by one definition only *possibilities* for future disasters. In a time dominated by complex technologies, massive increments in the rate of geologic and climatic interventions, and global political and social tensions, it is always a possibility that the type, scope, and intensity of future disasters may be unlike anything we have known in the past.

To avoid any misunderstanding, I find no difficulty in affirming that quantitative data on past disasters are generally quite useful for sensitizing hazards researchers to historical trends in levels of hazardousness and vulnerability—an approach sometimes referred to as the natural standards method, or "bootstrapping" (cf. Fischhoff et al. 1981, p. 50). I will look at some of this research shortly. But a genuinely critical interest in hazardousness and vulnerability cannot be entirely limited to these types of factual study. In bringing social theory to bear on the problems of hazardousness and vulnerability our concern must also be with the *critical evaluation of potentials and possibilities for harm and avoiding harm*. In short, as social investigators we must take a moral stand in the ongoing debate on the nature of hazards, even in the absence—and perhaps in the face—of available data. We shall see that the notions of potential harm and its avoidance are intimately tied to the question of the public detection of hazards raised in the last chapter, and that it is the essential task of a critical theory of hazards to unravel the relations between the conditions for public detection and changing levels of hazardousness and vulnerability.

My argument is essentially based on the following points which anticipate the more detailed analysis I will offer below.

First, *in principle*, a hazard must be detectable in order to count *as* a hazard. To posit an undetect*able*—in contrast to a simply undetect*ed*—hazard is a contradiction in terms. This may seem trivial at first glance, but since I expect this to be the most controversial claim of my thesis, I will spend some time trying to defend it.

Second, when a hazard goes undetected, it increases the degree of vulnerability to an accident, or conversely, decreases the ability to take individual or collective actions to plan for or respond effectively to an accident. Such actions will be provisionally characterized as "mitigations," and detection itself as one among the many possible forms of action that mitigation can take. For the most part, these are relatively uncontroversial positions in empirical hazards research.

Third, in speaking of detect*ability* or the *possibility* of detection, I am attempting to articulate a strategic point around which a uniquely critical theory of hazards can develop, and also to establish some conceptual distance from the traditional theory of *disasters*, which up to this time has been the major focus of sociological, as contrasted with geological, research. Detectability plays a relatively minor role in studies that are primarily concerned with the effects of disasters on social organization. But it is the conceptual cornerstone of any sociological theory of hazards, since such a theory must specify and critique socio-cultural processes that condition actors' perceptions of risk and safety. These processes are essentially prior in time to actual disasters. Many of the commonly used terms in contemporary hazards research—subjective and objective risk, risk-aversion and risk-taking, safety, potential harm, and mitigation—presuppose some conceptualization, either implicit or explicit, of the detection process. Without the aid of this concept, our theoretical field of inquiry literally disappears.

Fourth, all hazards are the outcome of complex interactions between technological, ecological, socio-political, and cultural systems. Although the conventional analytic distinction between natural (geological/climatological) and technological hazards is useful for a variety of practical purposes, in theory it is important to recognize that there are no purely "natural" hazards, just as there are, for example, no purely "industrial" accidents. In attempting to arrive at a *general* conceptualization of hazards, technical failures have no special status over geologic disturbances, or even sociopolitical conflicts.

Two Hypotheses

Despite the relative scarcity of data, two central hypotheses are now beginning to emerge and find some support in the field of hazards research— first, the increasing hazardousness of our everyday environment, and second, the heightened vulnerability of the poor and disadvantaged classes to those hazards whose outcome are actual disasters (cf. Burton et al. 1978, Chap. 1; Perrow 1984, Chap. 3; Wijkman and Timberlake 1984, pp. 27-32; White 1974, Chap. 1; Lagadec 1982, pp. 3-4). In this section, I propose to examine and critique some of the available evidence for both hypotheses, building initially upon definitions of hazardousness and vulnerability that are applicable to both natural and technological events. My interpretations are based primarily on extrapolations from occurrences of past disasters in which fatalities were involved. I must caution again, however, that I view such data as only marginally useful for illustrating the hazards process in general theoretical or critical terms.

Defining Hazardousness

Hazardousness is defined here simply as the potential to cause harm to persons. Most of the literature on hazards usually expresses this idea indirectly, emphasizing such factors as the probability of injury or loss of life (Burton et al. 1978, pp. 2-4; Gruntfest et al. 1978, p. 72), political and economic dislocation (Mileti et al. 1981, pp. 21-25; Palm 1985, p. 65; Dacy and Kunreuther 1969), or social-psychological dysfunctions associated with exposure to environmental threats (Baum et al. 1981, pp. 119-122; D'Souza 1980, pp. 29-42; Bates et al. 1963).

While each of these captures something of the idea of hazardousness, the concept of potential harm has the merit of being broad enough to encompass all specific refinements. Harm to persons need not, for instance, be strictly limited to actual bodily suffering or death. Persons may also be harmed when their homes, businesses, or fellow human beings are

TABLE 2.1 Number of persons killed per year in disasters

Type of Event	1960s	1970s
Drought	1,010	23,110
Flood	2,370	4,680
Civil strife/conflict	300	28,840
Tropical cyclone	10,750	34,360
Earthquake	5,250	38,970
Other disasters	2,890	12,960
TOTAL	22,570	142,920

Source: Anders Wijkman and Lloyd Timberlake, Natural Disasters: Acts of God or Acts of Man? Philadelphia: New Society Publishers. 1988, p. 23. Used by permission.

adversely affected by extreme events. To experience the negative impacts of all such events at an individual level, regardless of whether or not personal injury or death is the result, is to be harmed by these events.

Increasing Hazardousness

How do we determine whether the environment is becoming more or less hazardous, i.e., whether it exhibits an increasing or decreasing potential for inflicting personal harm? A standard procedure for determining the degree of hazardousness at a given time (or of a particular object, event, location or process) is to examine historical rates of casualties or other forms of loss to persons from disasters, or to focus on the rate of occurrence of disastrous events themselves and extrapolate this information in the form of trends to possible futures (Wijkman and Timberlake 1984, pp. 21–32; Burton et al. 1978, chap. 1; Hewitt and Burton 1971; White 1974, Chap. 1; Fischoff et al. 1981, p. 50ff.).[4] For "natural" hazards trends associated with floods, droughts, hurricanes, earthquakes, and the like, these types of statistics are relatively straightforward to interpret (Table 2.1). Over the last two decades, the Swedish Red Cross has estimated that total number of people killed in extreme geological and climatological events has risen almost sixfold, although this figure is somewhat less when the confusing

TABLE 2.2   Number of persons affected per year by disaster

Type of Event	1960s	1970s
Drought	18,500,000	24,400,000
Flood	5,200,000	15,400,000
Civil strife/conflict	1,100,000	4,000,000
Tropical Cyclone	2,500,000	2,800,000
Earthquake	200,000	1,200,000
Other disasters	200,000	500,000
TOTAL	27,700,000	48,300,000

Source: Anders Wijkman and Lloyd Timberlake, Natural Disasters: Acts of God or Acts of Man? Philadelphia: New Society Publishers. 1988, p. 24. Used by permission.

category "civil strife" is dropped from the calculation (Wijkman and Timberlake 1984). Considered by type of event, the general direction of increase holds but varies significantly, with droughts and earthquakes registering the greatest impact. The total number of persons affected, i.e., otherwise harmed economically or socially by these events over the same period has also dramatically increased (Table 2.2).

The number of actual recorded natural disasters also rose on average during the 1960s and 1970s (Table 2.3). These statistics do not reflect the mean number of geophysical or climatological "extremes" (abnormalities in the physical environment), which held relatively constant over this time frame, but only the number of events in which persons were actually killed, injured, or harmed in some manner or other.

With regard to technological or industrial hazards—which increase the likelihood of events such as chemical spills, explosions, irradiation from nuclear sources, etc.—the evidence is more difficult to interpret. Table 2.4 shows that twelve of the nineteen major industrial accidents in the twentieth century involving 100 or more deaths have occurred since 1950 (cf. Lagadec 1982; Shrivastava 1987; Kottary 1985, p. 8; Bowonder et al. 1985, p. 8). If one includes smaller scale incidents, transportation accidents, dam breaks and structural collapses in this total, the evidence for increasing hazardousness is more compelling (Lagadec 1982, pp. 147ff.).

TABLE 2.3 Number of recorded disaster events per year

Type of Event	1960s	1970s
Drought	5.2	9.7
Flood	15.1	22.2
Civil strife/conflict	4.1	6.8
Tropical cyclone	12.1	14.5
Earthquake	6.9	8.3
Other disasters	10.8	19.5
TOTAL	54.2	81.0

Source: Anders Wijkman and Lloyd Timberlake, Natural Disasters: Acts of God or Acts of Man? Philadelphia: New Society Publishers. 1988, p. 22. Used by permission.

Although both the number of actual events and the fatalities resulting from major industrial accidents are often smaller in comparison to the havoc wreaked by natural disasters, there are a number of reasons to think that future accidents will be both more numerous and larger in scale due to the increasing complexity or proneness to so-called "system failures" in these industries (cf. Perrow 1984, pp. 72–79). In the U.S. chemical industry alone between 1980 to 1984 there were 2051 reported injuries from all chemically-related accidents (Sorenson 1986, p. 5). Although this is a relatively low figure, the increasing rate of minor mishaps in this industry is disturbing, and the probability of a major disaster occurring in the U.S. sometime in the future cannot be ruled out. In Bhopal, in any case, the luck eventually ran out when at least 1,800 persons lost their lives.

Problems of Interpretation

What makes it difficult to give a straightforward interpretation to these figures is that both so-called natural and technological disasters have potentially long-term consequences that can affect life and health negatively and that are known only uncertainly (cf. Kates 1977, p. 11). It is an unresolved question how to include in the assessment of hazards persons who *may* die much later from their initial exposure to catastrophic events

TABLE 2.4 Major industrial disasters of the twentieth century[a]

Year	Accident	Site	Fatalities
1917	Factory explosion	Petrograd, USSR	100
1921	Chemical plant explosion	Oppau, Germany	561
1942	Coal dust explosion	China	1572
1942	Chemical plant explosion	Belgium	200
1944	Gas explosion	Cleveland, USA	136
1947	Fertilizer ship explosion	Texas City, USA	562
1948	Ether explosion	Ludwigshafen, Germany	245
1956	Mercury discharge	Minimata, Japan	250
1956	Dynamite explosion	Cali, Columbia	1100
1970	Gas explosion	Osaka, Japan	92
1975	Mine explosion	Chasnala, India	431
1978	Propylene explosion	Los Alfaques, Spain	216
1978	Natural gas explosion	Xilatopec, Mexico	100
1979	Chemical warfare accident	Novosibirsk, USSR	300
1980	Off-shore rig collapse	Norway	123
1982	Oil explosion	Tacoa, Venezuela	145
1984	Petrol explosion	Sao Paulo, Brazil	508
1984	Natural Gas explosion	Mexico City	452
1984	Poison gas leak	Bhopal, India	1800-10,000

[a]Accounting for more than 90 deaths each, not including transportation accidents, structural failures, or figures for personal injury.
Sources: Figures compiled from Lagadec 1982; Bowonder et al. 1985; Shrivastava 1987.

(or suffer permanent physical, economic, or social-psychological damages) (cf. Wijkman and Timberlake 1984, p. 23; Burton et al 1978, p. 96). The prospect for negative long-term effects from minor, routine hazards is even more difficult to assess. For example, future rates of cancer caused by exposure to low-level radiation or social losses associated with chemical pollution of the ecosystem are extremely difficult to project. In one study of chemical poisoning from pesticides, deaths in the Third World alone have been estimated at 22,000 per year and rising at an annual rate of five percent, but even this limited information probably does not reflect the extent of the problem (Gupta 1985, p. 151; see also Waldbott 1978; U.S. Council on Environmental Quality 1978; U.N. Environment Programme 1979; Rele 1985). Despite (and because of) these questions, there are compelling practical reasons for including such speculative data in evaluations of global hazardousness, not the least of which is that it forces us to take a more cautious and critical approach to the adoption and implementation of new technologies.

Defining Vulnerability

Statistics from the Third World regarding losses from disasters tend to support the second major hypothesis of hazards research, viz., the disproportionate vulnerability of the poorest social classes to the hazards of their environment. Vulnerability is defined here provisionally as an inability to take effective measures—hereafter referred to as "mitigations"—that would insure against losses from disaster or allow for efficient recovery. Such measures include evacuation and relocation plans, land use and siting regulations, technical redundancy measures, and structural improvements. In addition, I include in this set what I will call "first-order mitigations," viz., all actions taken to enhance basic possibilities for the detection of hazards (e.g., warning systems) (cf. Milliman 1982, p. 3; Mileti 1980, p. 327).

Previous studies of vulnerability have defined this concept in terms of a social system's viability, susceptibility, or proneness to risk in coping with the potential losses imposed by environmental extremes (Pelanda 1982, pp. 68–72; Lewis 1979, p. 104; Friedman 1975; Gabor and Griffith 1979, p. 325; Barkun 1977). Considered functionally, each of these terms refers to the capacity of a social system to recover from a catastrophic event and resume a relative degree of "normal" operation in the provision of basic goods and services. Possible recovery, in other words, depends to a large degree on the flexibility or adaptability of system organizations during times of catastrophe. If organizational flexibility is high, so the argument goes, the less vulnerable the system is to external or internal threats.

Functional explanation of this sort has been extensively criticized in the current theoretical literature for, among other reasons, uncritically transposing human traits to abstract entities such as social systems (in this case "flexibility") (cf. Giddens 1979). It is difficult to conceptualize the vulnerability of social systems without first assuming that this vulnerability also characterizes individuals, but the reverse of this is not necessarily true. Individuals may be vulnerable to hazards without this fact necessarily entailing a threat to the basic integrity of social systems. Thus, when speaking of vulnerability, it makes more sense to talk about the special problems of individuals or, at most and with appropriate caveats, social classes composed of individuals (cf. Wijkman and Timberlake 1984, p. 27; Pankhurst 1984, p. 206–208). Individuals are vulnerable to losses from disasters to the degree that they are unable to take protective (or avoidance) measures that would insure them against these losses. In short, vulnerability, considered as a property of individuals, is a consequence of the impossibility or improbability of effective mitigation.

Increasing Vulnerability

There is an increasing amount of evidence to suggest that to be poor means having a greater chance of dying in a disaster—natural or technological. There are over 3,000 deaths per natural disaster in low income countries on the average, but only 500 per event in high income countries (Wijkman and Timberlake 1984, p. 27; Hagman 1984; based on definitions of high and low income supplied by the World Bank). Table 2.5 breaks down this information further by type of economy, number of (natural) disaster events 1960–1981, and number of fatalities.

A number of other works in the natural hazards field lend support to the conclusion that the poor or disadvantaged suffer disproportionately more in disaster (cf. Friedsam 1962, pp. 164–176; Hutton 1976, p. 261; Perry et al. 1981; Perry et al. 1982, pp. 306–308; Sen 1981, Chap. 1; White and Haas 1975, pp. 181–193; Jefferey 1982). The evidence for enhanced vulnerability once again, however, becomes clouded when technological accidents are considered, both because these accidents are fewer in number than their natural counterparts (making any generalization difficult), and their long-term effects so uncertain. There is very little research, for example,

TABLE 2.5 Disasters and fatalities by type of economy

	Number of Disaster Events 1960-1981	Number of Fatalities
Low Income Economy		
Afghanistan	12	540
Bangladesh	63	633,000
Burma	26	1,500
Chad	14	2,300
China	20	247,000
Ethiopia	16	103,000
Gambia	11	200
Haiti	17	6,400
India	96	60,000
Laos	11	400
Madagascar	13	420
Mali	13	540
Mozambique	13	1,100
Nepal	19	2,900
Niger	12	320
Pakistan	21	7,400
Somalia	11	19,000
Sri Lanka	18	1,900
Sudan	11	310
Tanzania	12	590
Upper Volta	16	870
Vietnam	22	8,800
Middle Income Economy		
Algeria	20	3,800
Bolivia	21	530
Brazil	39	4,100
Chile	17	8,000
Costa Rica	16	70
Ecuador	21	640
Greece	15	190
Honduras	18	3,400
Hong Kong	10	860
Indonesia	59	17,000
Iran	38	48,000
Malaysia	19	310
Mexico	37	2,600
Nicaragua	17	106,000
Panama	11	100
Peru	31	91,000
Philippines	76	17,000
South Korea	27	2,900
Thailand	10	1,300
Turkey	33	12,000
Yugoslavia	14	5,100
High Income Economy		
Italy	24	6,100
Japan	43	2,700
Spain	12	1,900

Source: Anders Wijkman and Lloyd Timberlake, Natural Disasters: Acts of God or Acts of Man? Philadelphia. New Society Publishers. 1988, p. 28. Used by permission.

that would indicate long-term exposure to chemicals or radiation disproportionately impacts the poorest social classes (cf., however, arguments by
Norris 1982, Chap. 2; Gupta 1985; Lagadec 1982; Rele 1985). One does
not need long-term projections to know, however, that in Bhopal by far
the majority of persons killed were very poor and that the greatest number
of those who will suffer various future debilitating diseases from their
exposure to the poison gas are also poor (Bowonder et al. 1985, p. 7).
Data from other sources also shows—although more uncertainly—that the
majority of fatalities resulting from slow exposure to toxic pesticides are
incurred by poor farmers in the Third World who have had little experience
in the safe handling of chemicals (Norris 1982, Chap. 2; Mojumder 1985).

Limitations of Historical Data

Even taking into account the methodological problems involved in
projecting past disaster data into the future, there is an important theoretical
problem in using figures such as those given above to indicate hazardousness
at a given time (or for a given object/location/action) or the vulnerability
of individuals. While statistics gathered on loss of life or the frequency of
past disasters are obviously important (and, to a certain extent, inescapable)
in the analysis of hazards, it is crucial to grasp that not one *actual* person
need be harmed nor a single *actual* disaster occur for individuals to be
considered vulnerable or for something to constitute a hazard. I emphasize
the term "actual" because hazards truly exist only as "potentials" for
disasters or accidents and should never be confused with these latter terms.
Actual rates of loss, even when projected into an uncertain future, simply
do not adequately or completely capture this "potential" character of hazards.
It is precisely on this point that conventional bootstrapping methods for
investigating the hazards process are critically deficient.

The Possibility of Detection

A critical inquiry into the role of detection in establishing levels of
hazardousness and vulnerability is one alternative to relying solely on
historical rates of loss, and better suited to a notion of hazards as potentials.
I begin with a couple of hypotheses: if the possibility of detecting hazards
decreases, both the hazardousness of the environment and the vulnerability
of individuals or classes of individuals can be expected to increase (Fig.
2.1). Before examining these hypotheses in more detail, however, I first

FIGURE 2.1 Preliminary Model of the Hazards Process

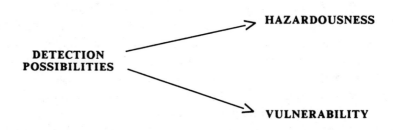

need to look more closely at what the "possibility of detection" means and how it is theoretically related to the concepts of hazard, mitigation, and vulnerability, and second, at some of the possible limitations of this type of analysis.

Detection, Mitigation, and Hazards— Theoretical Relations

Investigators have noted that a hazard must first be detected, i.e., seen as having the potential to cause harm, before further measures can be taken to neutralize it (cf. Mileti et al. 1985, p. 7; Mileti et al. 1981, p. 76). Detection can therefore be defined in a dual sense, both as a necessary (first-order) condition of subsequent mitigation efforts and as a type of mitigation itself. In its absence or failure, all preventative actions are automatically ruled out, and surviving a disaster becomes more or less a matter of luck. Emergency preparedness plans, zoning regulations, structural reinforcements, and other forms of mitigation ultimately depend upon this initial detection of the hazard. To further complicate matters, detection is itself contingent on prior factors. Even the awareness that something has a potential for causing personal harm, a factor long recognized in hazards research as important in motivating individuals to take protective action, ultimately depends on an *ability* to detect the hazard (cf. Mileti and Beck 1975, pp. 27–28). All hazards, whether natural or technological, must be "detectable" *in principle*. To detect a hazard means to recognize in a given phenomenon a certain potential for producing harm—literally to experience a time, event, object, location, action, etc., *as* a hazard. These phenomena lose their hazardous character if their potential dangers remain undetectable, which is to say that when all possibility of detection fails (as a limit case), the very term "hazard" loses its application.

An example will help to illustrate this idea. Consider the case of the blind and deaf person approaching a hole dug in the ground (ignore for now the important question of who dug this hole or for what purpose). S/he can neither see the hazard nor be informed verbally about its presence. The only opportunity to detect the hazard is by some other mechanism (a seeing eye dog, a warning delivered in braille, etc.). The limit case where not only these latter mechanisms fail, *but all possible mechanisms for all possible persons*, is the point at which the term "hazard" loses both its theoretical usefulness and its prospective or predictive value: the hazard cannot be recognized or evaluated until an actual accident happens (s/he stumbles into the hole), which is to say that the hazard is then known only retrospectively, after the damage has already been done. There is probably always some possibility of detecting a hazard in advance in everyday situations, no matter how small. But the closer we approach the theoretical and practical limit of no possibility of prior detection, the more we find ourselves constrained to using the vocabulary of "disasters" rather than the language of "hazards," and, significantly, the more we risk being harmed.

Environmental disturbances that disrupt the routine functioning of social relationships are known in the current hazards literature as "extreme events" (cf. Dynes 1970, Chap. 2; Burton et al. 1978, p. 1; Mileti 1980, p. 327). When possibilities of detection are systematically impoverished, these events come as a *surprise*—they surpass all our calculations and undermine the expectations we have built up from our past experience with disasters. In contrast to this, merely to be able to perceive that something is a hazard enhances, *prior to all calculation of the magnitude of risk*, the individual's chances to eliminate at least some of this surprise (Kates 1977, p. 12).[5] It is important to note that detection is an activity that the entire range of individuals or groups living with environmental hazards perform. It is not limited to scientists and emergency managers, but involves persons from all walks of life, and in all cultural settings. It is often the case, for example, that the initial detection of a hazard comes from private citizens or groups (Sorenson and Gersmehl 1980, pp. 130–131). Unfortunately, such was not the case in Bhopal. There we have seen that residents crowded around Union Carbide's pesticide facility were virtually unaware of the hazard, i.e., *for them* it was not only undetected but to a large degree undetectable. This lack of the necessary conditions for awareness, which put many of them in the position of having to assume involuntary risks, was a crucial factor in accounting for the terrible death toll from the accident (*New York Times* 1985d).[6]

Detection and Vulnerability— Theoretical Relations

For similar reasons, vulnerability to hazards is not adequately conceptualized until it is tied to the possibility of detection. To be sure, any number of factors may contribute to making individuals vulnerable, including their spatial proximity to hazards (Diggory 1956, p. 47), their age or physical characteristics (Hutton 1976, p. 261; Pankhurst 1984, pp. 206–209), or their potential to recover from the effects of disaster, their organizational or material means of response (Pelanda 1982), and, not least, their socio-economic class standing. Important as all of these factors are, however, it is only when the possibility of detection is absent that individuals become vulnerable to hazards in the strongest and most basic sense, viz., the sense of becoming potential and unwitting *victims*. It can, of course, be argued that persons deprived of the material resources for relocating away from hazardous areas or for developing emergency plans that enable them to cope in spite of their age, disability, and recovery problems are also in some basic sense "vulnerable." Certainly the necessity of material resources is incontestable. *But resources for relocation or emergency planning are moot points if possibilities for detecting hazards are, prior to an actual disaster, unavailable.*

I do not wish to belabor this point unduly, for the argument can be reversed: material resources are also necessary to enhance possibilities of detection. Information regarding hazards always has its costs, at least initially, and near the end of this chapter I will focus in more detail on the theoretical and practical significance of the issue of resources for the hazards process. Still, in Bhopal it is clear that residents were vulnerable primarily because they were never informed, or badly informed, of the hazards of living in such close proximity to Union Carbide's pesticide plant, of how to act in case of an emergency, or how to gain compensation for their losses (Bowonder et al. p. 7; Sharma and Singh 1985; Ramaseshan 1985a). Given the well-documented phenomena of corporate and bureaucratic secrecy, such information could not readily have been purchased even had adequate resources been available to residents for that purpose. For this reason I will assign a specific theoretical priority to the problem of the social control of information and its consequences for the public perception of hazards, even though I realize that practically speaking the issue of material resources is of comparable importance.

Limitations of the Analysis

Thus, while the possibility of detection is a necessary condition of mitigation and hence also a necessary element in contributing to rising levels of hazardousness and vulnerability, it is never claimed to be sufficient. The possibility of detecting a hazard does not and cannot imply that appropriate or necessary actions to enhance safety will be undertaken subsequent to detection. Even had the residents of Bhopal detected the hazards at Union Carbide's pesticide facility in advance, a host of other constraints undoubtedly operated to limit their capacity to respond effectively to those hazards—limited access to transportation, non-existent telephone service, confused warnings, to name just a few (Diamond 1985a). Many of the residents of the small bastis surrounding the plant were also already somewhat physically debilitated and therefore an easy target for the poison gas that entered their homes on the night of December 2nd, 1984 (Dehli Science Forum 1985).

The possibility of detection is central only in the sense that it forms a *paradigm* for the critical analysis of hazards—an exemplary tool for constructing not only a theory of hazards, but for organizing practical activity as well. Again: lacking the possibility of detection, all else *fails*—finding transportation, issuing warnings, etc.—all of the things that could have been done in Bhopal to save lives. The critical questions this book originally posed about hazardousness and vulnerability can now be further refined: what social strategies and processes contributed to the limitation of the possibility for detecting hazards at Bhopal? On what social and political levels—global, corporate, state, and private—did these processes operate? What, if anything, can the Bhopal tragedy tell us about detection and the hazards process in general and about possible ways to reestablish some degree of public control over this process?

I will take a non-traditional, controversial, and explicitly critical approach to these questions. This approach involves an argument for the proposition that "hazard" and "mitigation" are, in the final analysis, *interchangeable* terms, and that the same "objective" condition (event/object/action/location/ time) can be fully described and analyzed under either (or both) labels, depending on whose perspective one chooses to adopt. Simply stated, at the level of their possible description, all hazards are mitigations, and all

mitigations are hazards. Hazards are then rendered detectable (or undetectable) by *definitional* strategies designed to enhance perceptions of relative
harm (or safety) and which are motivated by specific political and economic
interests.

I alluded to this possibility briefly in the last chapter. I argued in that
chapter that, for groups composed of coalitions of experts, corporate
managers, and state officials, the hazards associated with pesticides production in Bhopal were redefined in such as way as to focus attention
exclusively on their mitigative potential, i.e., by stressing the beneficial
function of chemical manufacturing for increasing Third World food supplies
and providing economic stability through the modernization of agricultural
practices. From an opposing perspective, however, it is precisely the mitigative potential of pesticides production that provided the ideological
justification for the development and export of such a "hazardous" industry
to the Third World in the first place.

This always conceivable reversal in the application of the terms "hazard"
and "mitigation" takes place within the context of an ongoing *political
struggle* over just whose definition of the hazards process will win out,
i.e., which definitions of relative safety or acceptable risk will emerge and
prevail. In Bhopal, prior to December 2nd, 1984, technocratic definitions
of the risks associated with pesticides production held sway, and this most
likely contributed to narrowing the possibilities for detecting a number of
hazards at Carbide's facility and potentially saving many lives during the
actual accident (Ramaseshan 1985a; Ramaseshan 1985b). On the other
hand, much of the commentary that has emerged in the press and the
hazards literature in the wake of the accident—my own included—has
tended to side with its victims. It has adopted a perspective that is openly
critical of an ideology that legitimates the export of hazardous materials
to the Third World in the name of mitigation.

Redefining Hazards and Mitigations

I will now attempt to formalize these somewhat diverse observations in
terms of a provisional model of discursive processes which constrain the
detection of hazards. In the following chapter, I will expand this model
to include economic and cognitive factors that limit the possibilities for
detecting hazards and explain how this limitation increases the overall
hazardousness of the socio-physical environment in addition to enhancing
the vulnerability of the poor to those hazards.

All hazards carry the potential to be redefined as mitigations and all mitigations—actions to reduce the potentially disruptive consequences of hazards—are themselves capable of being redefined as hazards. For the moment, I state this only as an initial hypothesis regarding the interchangeability or substitutability of these two terms, for although this linking of hazards to mitigations in the workings of symbolic/sign systems is implicit in some of the hazards literature (cf. Douglas and Wildavsky 1982; White 1974; Sussman et al. 1983), as far a I am aware it has never been fully explored. In line with this hypothesis, I propose the following formal definitions.

A hazard is a potential failure in the mitigation or system of mitigations that is designed to nullify an object, event, location or action's ability to cause harm to persons. Conversely, a mitigation is any social technology designed to enhance safety, but whose potential failure within a system of mitigations itself constitutes a hazard.

These two definitions have in common the concept of a "potential failure." In order to gain an idea of the importance of this concept for what follows, let us imagine a hypothetical case.

Company X has operated a chemical facility in close proximity to a major urban center for the past ten years. During that time, there were several occasions when production was temporarily suspended because of minor breakdowns or mishaps that resulted in toxic materials being released. None of these releases, however, caused any visible or lasting harm, thanks to an extremely efficient system of backup safety systems and emergency procedures that had been designed and implemented by the company during the construction of the plant. In addition, the company manufactured chemical products in similar facilities in various locations throughout the world with the same admirable safety record. Based on their past experience, therefore, the company's representatives were able to claim with a high degree of confidence that any threat posed by their operations could be effectively countered.

A minimum amount of reflection shows, however, that past experience in the successful containment of hazards is itself never an absolute guarantee of future safety. *Even the smallest hazard can serve as a warning.* The most hardened believer in the merits of technology is forced to admit that no mitigation can be designed so efficiently that it will take into account all possible contingencies. Mitigation is a form of rational action—more precisely, a type of *instrumental* action undertaken to achieve a calculable end (safety) through the calculated choice of means—and all forms of instrumental action are potentially fallible, even if the probability of failure is infinitesimally small (cf. Habermas 1984, Chap. 1). It is precisely the attribution of an inherent fallibility to instrumental forms of action that enables us to say that mitigations are in themselves hazardous, as opposed to saying that mitigations merely *contain* hazards within acceptable boundaries. Perfect mitigation, were it possible in some ideal sense, would essentially render the notion of a hazard meaningless, since totally efficient (i.e., infallible) mitigation would imply the complete elimination of the hazard. From this perspective, imperfect mitigation in effect is what constitutes, or defines, the nature and possibility of the hazard. In identifying or detecting a hazard, we must point precisely to the potential failure of the mitigative systems that are designed to "contain" the threat. Thus for all its widely publicized safety systems (and precisely because of the fallibility of these systems), Union Carbide of India's pesticide plant in Bhopal can be legitimately described as a hazard. And this is true regardless of the past safety record of the plant or the company's operations prior to the actual accident.

This line of reasoning reiterates a key point. Hazards should not be mistaken for the physical events that actually produce loss or damage. Insofar as they are the products of complex interactions among social, natural, and technological systems, hazards exist prior to damage-causing events. The latter, as physical phenomena abstracted from their social context, are, as noted, normally referred to as "extremes" in the literature (Wijkman and Timberlake 1984, p. 11; Mileti 1980, p. 327). The point that hazards exist only as potentials for harm cannot be overemphasized. A hazard is no more than an accident *waiting to happen*; it is not the accident itself. Thus, on this definition, an actual earthquake does not constitute a hazard. Living on a fault line in a structure unable to withstand an earthquake does, however, constitute a hazard since the design of earthquake resistant structures, along with zoning regulations intended to limit building along fault lines, are potentially fallible methods of responding to the threat of an earthquake. Similarly, the release of toxic materials from a chemical plant, considered solely as a physical event, is not a hazard according to the above definitions. But a faulty warning light (detection mechanism) within the plant or an inadequate warning system outside do constitute hazards, insofar as in possibly failing they create a potential for harm. Placed within a sufficiently large context such as the global ecosystem, we can and often do portray the chemical industry itself as a hazard. This becomes possible when the mitigative effects that are claimed to flow from the industry-wide production of chemicals (e.g., increasing aggregate food supplies and decreasing numbers of agricultural pests) are set against the potentially negative long range effects of chemicals on the socio-physical environment (Rele 1985; Norris 1982, Chap. 2).

Thresholds of Fallibility

If all mitigations are potentially fallible, it is also a fact that some mitigations are more fallible than others. Some mitigations have, in other words, lower thresholds of fallibility depending, among other things, on their level of complexity. Perrow (1984, pp. 75–76) has noted that highly interactive systems of mitigation have increased the hazardousness of some production technologies to catastrophic levels. Interactive systems are those which generate unfamiliar and unexpected production sequences that are so tightly linked by complex lines of feedback and redundancy that it becomes exceedingly difficult to intervene in the system in order to stop a chain of potentially catastrophic reactions. A number of modern productive technologies, such as nuclear power, space weapons systems, and chemical facilities have these properties. Perrow has argued convincingly, for example, that the accident at Three Mile Island was an example of system complexity overriding human efforts to understand and halt the progressive failures that took place during the accident.

Perrow's notion of highly interactive, and hence highly fallible, systems of mitigation is an important explanation for the increasing hazardousness of the environment, and it fits well with the analysis I am developing here. But while it explicitly alludes to the fact that mitigations may be hazardous, Perrow tends to overstate the purely technical side of this—mitigations become hazards at some ill-defined point where rational-instrumental sophistication outpaces human control.[7] A technical approach to hazards is useful for the purpose for which it is intended, viz., as a critique of unduly complex technologies—it says that we must opt for simpler, more linear, and more flexible productive techniques (both in terms of machinery and social organization). I have no argument with this. On the other hand, I think the problem lies at a much deeper and more profound level, viz., the level on which instrumental techniques have themselves become universal means for defining and manipulating the very perception of relative risk and safety. In adhering to a more or less technical line of argument, Perrow undertheorizes the cultural and political dimensions involved in the discursive transformation of mitigations into hazards and hazards into mitigations. I do not believe, therefore, that Perrow's otherwise insightful critique of technological sophistication is sufficiently radical.

The inevitable academic controversies that are spawned by analyses like Perrow's point to the fact that the theory of hazards is, in the final analysis, both a *scientific and political discourse,* and within this discourse the concept of "hazard" can substitute just as easily for the concept of "mitigation" (when the latter's fallibility becomes the focus) as the concept of "mitigation" can substitute for the concept of "hazard" (by the argument that the hazard constitutes an acceptable risk, i.e., that while warning us to its potential dangers it also delivers benefits that outweigh its costs, however these latter two terms are defined).

It is easy to think of examples that illustrate this process. A pesticide plant may be seen as both a hazard (because of its potential to release toxic materials) and a mitigation (as an acceptable risk to insure against food shortages). A flood control device, such as a dam, is both a hazard (because of its potential for structural failure) and a mitigation (to protect against the cyclic effects of drought). Famine relief efforts are both a hazard (they may create dependency in relief recipients) and a mitigation (they prevent people from starving). A piece of broken glass on the sidewalk is a hazard (someone walking barefoot may cut himself) and a mitigation (someone, on seeing it, may remember it's a good idea to wear shoes outside). Finally, the process of detection itself may be both hazard and mitigation. I hinted in Chapter 1 that adequate detection of hazards at Union Carbide's facility in Bhopal on the part of the public might have threatened the Indian government's interest in insuring needed supplies of agricultural commodities and employment, not to mention Union Carbide's interest in operating a profitable industry. Had detection of the pesticide facility's safety problems been the dominant concern prior to the accident, there might have been a good chance the facility itself would have been shut down and the accident never have occurred (cf. Gaya 1985).

Hazard-Mitigation Transformations and Detection

The detection of hazards therefore is a process conditioned by cultural, political, and economic values. If they are to maintain and enhance their image among clients and constituency as providers of the public good, corporate enterprises and government must take account of how industrial hazards are perceived by the public (Ramaseshan 1984a; Ramaseshan 1984b; Leaning and Keyes 1984, Introduction). There is no consumer demand for hazards per se, just as, strictly speaking, no one "accepts" risks (Fischhoff et al. 1981, p. 3). Consumers, voters, and other relevant constituencies need to be convinced by some means or other not only to see certain risks as acceptable or perhaps even inevitable, but to *desire* these risks because taking them is in their own interest. An effective method of upholding the corporate image and sustaining demand is first to redefine a hazard as a mitigation embodying a limited degree of risk (or, more radically, to completely define the hazard away by denying all risks involved in mitigation). In Bhopal, for instance, individual consumers of chemical products were continually subjected to claims that these products were not only safe, but that any risks involved were acceptable in light of known benefits (Sharma and Singh 1985). But this means that transforming the perception of hazards into mitigations is not just an automatic and simple matter of redefinition. It involves a strategy or set of strategies for overcoming (potential) public resistance to a threat, for changing perceptions and beliefs through the fine political art of persuasion (cf. Perry et al. 1980, p. 133). While such strategies may initially be based upon the best of intentions, they can have the unintended effect of inducing a general feeling of security where none, perhaps, is justified.

Persuasion Through Setting Thresholds—An Example

Several authors have noted that effective response to hazards is conditional on individuals beliefs that a threat will produce actual harm if no action is taken to counter it (cf. Mileti and Beck 1975; Mileti 1980; Perry et al. 1981). Such beliefs cannot arise spontaneously, however, and depend, among other factors, on the detection of actual threatening cues from the environment or the persuasiveness of warning information designed to convey the seriousness of the threat. In the latter case, when such information is not forthcoming—either because this information is deliberately withheld to further certain interests or because the possibility for obtaining such information is not initially built into the system of detection—detection capabilities are limited and hazards are open to being redefined as acceptable risks.

The nuclear power industry provides an informative example of how hazards and mitigations are discursively transformed by state and corporate techniques of persuasion. Nuclear power generation is often presented by state officials and utility managers as a mitigation against dwindling supplies of domestic fossil fuels and the resulting need to rely on foreign imports. But it is, of course, plainly recognized that nuclear power poses serious, perhaps even catastrophic, potentials for disaster (Lovins 1979). The question of whether nuclear power production will come to be legitimately perceived more as a mitigation than a hazard depends a great deal on the politics of establishing a threshold of risk for nuclear power. Perrow (1984, pp. 47–48) notes that a recent *Nuclear Safety* report, despite listing page after page of accidents at nuclear plants throughout the country, was able to use these accidents as evidence that the system of mitigations was functioning properly—a case of "we've never had a major accident, so the system must be safe." The real problem, however, is whether the threshold of risk for nuclear power has been defined so high, viz., the catastrophic release of radiation over a populated area, that the preponderance of lower level failures and checks actually makes the overall productive system appear safe. By the action of setting a threshold, which itself involves a form of detection, the paradoxical result is obtained that the possibility of detecting the hazard at lower levels has been effectively compromised. Further, establishing this threshold as legitimate was something that could have been done only through the political interaction and negotiation of corporate managers, government officials, environmentalists, potential victims, and the like. It is never, strictly speaking, an exclusively scientific procedure, but involves a complex interplay of social values and their tradeoffs. For all the myths that surround the weight of scientific knowledge on questions of technical hazards, scientists are themselves no more than one more group of players—although an extremely influential group—in the game of defining hazards.

The Hazard-Mitigation Transformation System

A theoretical generalization can be made from such examples. The process of defining hazards and the legitimation of thresholds extends to all levels of what I term the "hazard/mitigation system." I define this system as the set of possible discursive transformations—from hazards to mitigations and vice versa—associated with a particular production technology. Figure 2.2 provides a simplified model of such a system. I develop this model here in order to provide an explicit logical framework within which the more substantive sociological considerations to be developed in Chapter 3 may be understood.

FIGURE 2.2 Hazard/Mitigation Transformation System

	HAZARD	MITIGATION	
GENERAL			
Potential failures in production technology	H_1 ⟵————————⟶M_1		Economic development/ political stability
	H_2 ⟵————————⟶M_2		
	H_3 ⟵————————⟶M_3		
Potential structural failures/ failures in social preparedness	H_4 ⟵————————⟶M_4		Building codes/evacuation plans/warning systems
	H_5 ⟵————————⟶M_5		
Potential component failures	H_n ⟵————————⟶M_n		Component failure safeguards (redundancies)
SPECIFIC			

Any system of hazards or mitigations can be ordered for heuristic purposes along a continuum from general to specific. By the terms general and specific, I have in mind an idea similar to Perrow's (1984, p. 70) when he speaks of distinguishing technological accidents in terms of component versus system failures. Component failures involve one or more failures in parts, units, or subsystems of a production process that have been designed for safety purposes, e.g., a faulty shut-off valve, gauge, pump, monitor, warning siren, etc. Once again, in the interests of developing a theoretically informed critique of hazards, I am concerned here not so much with actual failures as in the potential for such components to fail. Such potential failures—assuming they were isolated and not additive— would produce fairly specific (i.e., localized) spatial or temporal effects, i.e., they would not constitute hazards that might threaten the "viability" of an entire productive system or cause potential harm to large numbers of persons. On the other hand, Perrow also speaks of "system" failures, viz., failures that involve multiple components and threaten the general integrity of an entire production process with potentially catastrophic results.

In distinction to Perrow, I do not propose a simple typology of (potential) failures but a continuum along which potential failures have increasingly broad and long range effects. Fig. 2.2 provides some possible examples of different levels of hazards and mitigations along this continuum. I also do not wish to limit the analysis of hazards to potential failures in mechanical technologies but wish to consider also fallibility in things such as social preparedness measures and social policies designed to implement hazardous technologies. When Perrow speaks of system failures, he generally confines himself to the level of production facilities, such as chemical plants or nuclear reactors. My conception of the hazards system is broader, including potential failures in global mitigative strategies (modernization, development) and in overall productive technologies themselves. In other words, for technological forms of hazard, I am concerned with potential failures of entire *industries* and not solely with problems found in individual plants. The latter concerns are valid, of course, as the Bhopal case aptly illustrates. But they are fairly specific concerns when considered from the perspective of the hazardousness of the entire chemical industry.

In the upper left hand corner of Fig. 2.2, potential failures in overall production technologies pose hazards at the most general level. In examining chemical production at this level, we would be concerned with the broadest possible consequences to the socio-physical environment, e.g., long-term problems stemming from gradual pollution of the ecosystem, health problems to future generations from exposure to toxic materials and the like. But if hazards can also be redefined in terms of mitigative effects, we must also focus on potential long-term benefits of chemical production, viz., increases in overall supplies of food and the economic self-sufficiency and political stability that an adequate food supply helps to bring about. These factors are the (fallible) mitigative aspects of chemical production at the highest level of generality, and are represented in Fig. 2.2 in the upper right hand corner. All this would be followed by an analysis of potential failures whose effects are more specific. Such failures would presumably have more immediate than long range consequences, although losses resulting from such failures could also be quite catastrophic. The high casualty rates at Bhopal, for example, can be traced at this level of analysis to the lack of adequate warnings during the accident, the neglect of available evacuation guidelines, and policies regarding the location of the plant itself in a heavily populated region of India (Bowonder et al. 1985, p. 7).

Finally, at the lowest levels in Fig. 2.2, we are concerned like Perrow with specific component failures. At Bhopal, there were many small scale failures in relatively isolated mitigation units from the time the plant was originally licensed—again, faulty valves and warning lights, periodic shutdowns in the refrigeration system designed to keep chemicals at safe temperatures, flawed backup systems (redundancies), and low levels of worker training for emergencies. In the final analysis, all of these relatively specific failures combined to produce the tragedy, but before the actual accident such failures were perceived to be relatively isolated events that at most threatened only select individuals who worked in the plant. These failures are represented in Fig. 2.2 in the lower left and right hand corners of the diagram.

The connecting arrows in Fig. 2.2 indicate that "hazards" and "mitigations" as general descriptive terms are interchangeable. At the most specific levels, various safety components at the Bhopal plant were intentionally designed as mitigations against the possibility of chemical spills, but because of their potential for failure, they also posed and defined the degree of hazard associated with that level of mitigation. Had these devices functioned perfectly, and continued to function perfectly in an absolutely reliable manner, there would have been no hazard at Bhopal. Precisely because we are concerned here with potentials and not actual failures, whether these components are conceived of as hazards or mitigations is a matter of social definition and political legitimation. Once failure actually does occur, the question of whether or not a particular component or set of components was "really" a hazard becomes retrospective rather than prospective. This process of transformation takes place between all levels of the system.

Some Limitations

All this represents a fairly static analysis of the symbolic process through which hazards and mitigations are capable of having their cognitive content modified. To offer a complete illustration of this process, one would have to include the element of time. Categories and levels in Fig. 2.2 are in a continual process of definition and redefinition as new knowledge becomes available or new hazards detectable. Over the past decade, for example, the construction of new nuclear plants in the United States has come to a virtual halt as what was once a mitigation in the general sense of increasing energy supplies became redefined in the political arena as a hazard, i.e., an unacceptable risk (cf. Nuclear Regulatory Commission 1984). Pollution from the combustion of fossil fuels, considered unacceptable several years ago, is increasingly becoming more acceptable both to corporations and the general public as the search for alternate forms of energy continues (Elster 1983, Appendix 1). As this book is being written, litigation from the Bhopal accident is perhaps fundamentally changing attitudes regarding the safety of the chemical industry, especially in the Third World.

The Logic of Hazards Mitigation as an Explanation for Increasing Hazardousness and Vulnerability

In this final section, I wish to examine how an analysis of the discursive logic of hazard-mitigation transformations is useful for explaining variations in the possibility of detection, and how the latter can act to change levels of hazardousness and vulnerability among the poor. The argument turns on a recognized anomaly in the field of hazards research—the phenomenon that the rate of loss in disasters continues to rise in spite of ever more concentrated efforts by all concerned parties—corporations, governments, private individuals and groups—to mitigate these losses. If mitigation in general can be shown to be implicated in these losses, a case can also be made for the more specific hypothesis that detection itself, as a paradigm case of mitigation, plays a role in increasing hazardousness and vulnerability.

An Anomaly in Hazards Research

A puzzling finding in hazards research is that heightened vulnerability and hazardousness sometimes appears to be correlated with a rising trend in the implementation and rationalization of mitigation. That is, more persons now are potential victims of disaster even as our means for preventing disaster becomes more sophisticated. Gilbert White (1974, p. 3), one of the pioneers in natural hazards research, observed years ago the rather disturbing fact that increasing federal expenditures for flood management actually appeared to be associated with rising losses from flooding.[8] Although White's research was confined mainly to the United States and indicated that losses were generally rising only with respect to property and not to life, the implication that mitigation as a rational intervention in the environment could have disvalued consequences for hazardousness and vulnerability was not lost on those investigating the skyrocketing fatality rates from disasters in the Third World. Today, critics of global industrialization and modernization speculate that our large scale intervention in ecological processes, ostensibly to mitigate the potential for future disasters, has in part been responsible for this rise in casualties (Wijkman and Timberlake 1984, pp. 23–24; Hagman 1984; Tinker 1984). How can this be so?

Perrow (1984) has attempted, quite plausibly, to explain this paradox by suggesting that the design of mitigative systems has become so over-whelmingly complex that the potential for controlling hazardous processes has diminished at the same time that the technical means for detecting these processes has increased.[9] The more we know, the less we can do; the more we do, the less we know—and thus the greater dangers we expose ourselves to. But Perrow bypasses the role of language in all this—no attention is given to the discursive logic that, prior to the implementation of technical safeguards, enables hazards to be *identified* with mitigations. Within the broad framework of this logic, which is at its foundation a deeply embedded *cultural logic of harm and safety*, the use of the concept of complexity is itself only one of many possible strategies by which such identifications can be made. I will have occasion to examine these strategies in more detail in Chapter 3. For now, we can inquire into the general nature of this logic and how it is better suited to explain the aforementioned anomaly.

The Logic of Transformation and the Possibility of Detection

Studies dealing with the response of individuals to an environmental threat have noted that effective mitigation depends upon the perception of the threat as *real* (cf. Perry et al. 1981, Chap. 1; Perry and Mushkatel 1984, p. 29). If information concerning potential losses from an impending disaster is not believed, evacuation or other protective measures are not likely to be implemented and vulnerability is thus heightened through inaction. But, as I have argued, the belief in potential harm itself is contingent on the ability to detect an object, event, location, etc., *as* a hazard. If, on the other hand, a hazard has itself been rendered undetectable by redefining it as a mitigation—and I maintain all hazards can be redefined in this way—belief in personal *harm* is no longer the relevant theoretical consideration. Rather, it is a belief in personal *safety* that is now the question. The conditions of detection may also change the nature of this belief.

If one believes s/he is safe and bases this belief on the protective rather than hazardous character of existing mitigations, the result is likely to be inaction and enhanced vulnerability. In other words, vulnerability may be heightened by a belief that adequate safeguards are already in place to counter a particular threat—the threshold of hazardousness is perceived to be high. There are many examples of this type of effect in the literature. If, following White, it is believed that flood control structures are adequate protection against losses from flooding, settlement in areas prone to flooding may be indirectly encouraged because the hazards posed by these structures are no longer fully detectable as hazards—at least until a major flood overwhelms them (cf. White 1945). Leaning and Keyes (1984, Chap. 1) have noted that belief in the effectiveness of crisis relocation in the event of a nuclear war may actually encourage the possibility of a nuclear confrontation by giving a false sense of invulnerability. Many of the poor in Bhopal were never given any reason to believe their safety was at stake since most had little idea of what kinds of materials for what purpose were being produced at Union Carbide's factory (Diamond 1985a). The implication of these examples is that a belief in the potential for harm can be offset by a belief in the effectiveness or *nonhazardousness* of mitigations designed to cope with this potential. But if mitigations are themselves hazards, in virtue of their potential for failure, overall hazardousness and vulnerability may increase despite (and, significantly, *because of*) enhanced perceptions of safety. By this same token, the system can become more hazardous at the same time that it is perceived to be becoming less so, both conditions being functions of adding mitigations whose hazard potential is unseen.

With this in mind, we return to one of our original problems—enhanced hazardousness and the vulnerability of the world's poor to losses from disaster. There have been many reasons offered to explain this. The poor tend to live in dwellings that are structurally unsuited to withstand the impact of environmental extremes (Wijkman and Timberlake 1984, pp. 87–89). They often lack ready access to information concerning hazards that would be instrumental in providing for more timely evacuation (Hutton 1976). The poor are unable to afford insurance protection that would allow for recovery of losses following disaster (Wijkman and Timberlake 1984, Chap. 7). Finally, in many parts of the world, the poor are forced to live in locations that are often in closest proximity to hazards, where land values are lowest, such as areas prone to recurrent drought or surrounding industrial sites (Ramaseshan 1985a).

These class-specific deficiencies have direct implications for mitigation. To the extent that the poor lack the resources for effective mitigation on their own, they must rely on state sponsored mitigations designed to reduce their overall vulnerability. In wealthier countries, these mitigations include regulations on the structural design of buildings, social disaster insurance, land use plans, and a host of other actions involving such things as relief efforts after a disaster and education programs before (cf. Milliman 1982, p. 5).

Considered at a middle or specific level of the hazard/mitigation continuum (see Fig. 2.2), each of these safeguards is arguably effective in reducing the potential for social losses from disaster. In wealthier countries, for example, there is some evidence to suggest that improvements in the design of integrated warning and detection systems can reduce the number of casualties resulting from extremes in the environment (Anderson 1969, pp. 96–98).

But even in wealthier nations, aggregate figures indicating reduced casualties can be misleading. Specific mitigations designed to protect overall populations may actually have a higher potential for failure among low income groups. For example, warnings are effective only to the degree that they are heard and understood or to the extent that action can be taken upon receipt of the warning message (cf. Mileti 1980, p. 332; Perry and Mushkatel 1984, p. 33). But various low income groups (ethnic minorities, the physically or mentally handicapped, etc.) may not speak the language in which the warning is delivered, may not own the radios or televisions over which warnings usually come, or may lack access to transportation to evacuate a threatened area (cf. Hutton 1976, pp. 261–262).

In wealthier nations these group specific vulnerabilities to mitigation failure may be remedied, if only because the resources are available to further refine the system of safeguards in order to extend it to the poor. But, following Perrow, the dilemma with this approach lies in increasing the technical and organizational complexity of the mitigation system. If too many organizations become involved in the administration of mitigation programs, the failure of any one organization to meet its obligations in times of disaster may result in the failure of the overall system. When such failures occur, the burden is inevitably shifted once again to the poor.

General mitigation policies—those concerned not so much with things like warning, evacuation, or preparedness measures, but with things like long term food and energy supplies—also are important to consider in analyzing hazardousness and vulnerability among the poor. The interactive, systemic nature of general mitigation policies is both particularly evident and acute in low income countries. To take an agricultural example, the intense need for food and energy in these countries, due in large part to population pressures, has led to the deforestation of large areas. The general policy of clearing forests has provided much needed wood to meet immediate energy requirements and has made land available for agricultural purposes, but it has also altered watershed patterns and decreased the ability of soils to absorb or divert water. In the long run, this mitigation practice has thus increased the potential for catastrophic flooding (Wijkman and Timberlake 1984, 53–57). In the absence of more specific mitigations to protect the poor of these countries against periodic floods, losses have been mounting.

Increasingly, poor nations have turned to modern Western technologies to reduce the pressures of energy and food shortages. But, as the recent tragedy in Bhopal has demonstrated, the potential failure of these technologies may have catastrophic effects. The adoption of technological fixes for social problems in poor nations has not in general been accompanied by the systematic refinement of the specific mitigation efforts that have lowered short term losses to vulnerable groups in wealthier countries. But even here, as I have argued, the adoption or refinement of specific mitigations is no guarantee for the long run safety of the poor. Any mitigation, at any level of the continuum, poses some degree of risk. To be poor means to accept a disproportionate share of that risk.

A central reason for this is that the poor, over and above (yet certainly also because of) their lack of material resources, have been more thoroughly and systematically misled than any other social class as to the nature of the risks they face. In the face of the unexpected and with little information to challenge their belief in personal safety, they are left with no alternatives for protective action. Rather, their situation is one of inaction—the worst form of vulnerability—and not because they are unsophisticated or uneducated, but because they are *excluded*. Because the poor have the least access to information about hazards, they do not enter into most public decisions on such things as the construction of nuclear plants or the production of chemicals and their use in agriculture. In short, they do not participate at the highest levels in the definition of hazards, how mitigations themselves pose hazards, or how exposure to hazards might be justified by the long-term benefits they may promise.

Specific mitigation efforts often tend to treat the symptoms rather than the causes of hazardousness and vulnerability. For both economic and political reasons, we generally choose to implement better warning systems than call for the elimination of whole industries, for example. When these specific mitigations demonstrate their potential to fail and become hazards themselves, as occasionally they must over the long run, the poor are left with little or nothing in the way of resources to fall back on. When relief efforts come to a halt because of political conflicts, the poor can be left in states of heightened dependency (Wijkman and Timberlake 1984, pp. 108–112). When a drought blocks the production of agricultural export commodities (designed to safeguard a nation's economic viability), the poorest farmers find it impossible to make the switch back to subsistence agriculture. And when basic detection mechanisms fail at a chemical production facility, as they did in Bhopal, it is the people who live closest to the industrial site—the poor—who suffer the highest casualties.

Increasing hazardousness and vulnerability are thus phenomena that reveal themselves only by an analysis of *total* discursive systems which construct the boundaries of potential harm. Potential harm is the result of decision processes whose strategy is to redefine the introduction of hazards as mitigations at the most general levels, i.e., the level of industries and the social policies designed to control those industries. But the burden of hazardousness and vulnerability falls disproportionately on those having the least ability to detect hazards and the fewest resources to cope with potential losses. The poor lack the power to implement appropriate mitigations at even the most specific levels of the hazard/mitigation system. This is not to suggest that low income classes, given sufficient power, would redefine the hazard/mitigation system in such as way as to reduce their own specific vulnerability. It is only to suggest that the poor are subject to a political and symbolic process of definition that acts to make their detection of hazards in the socio-physical environment considered as a total system more difficult and limited. In Chapter 3, I propose to examine these processes in more detail by relating them to general theoretical concerns within sociology.

Conclusion

To summarize: at a global level, hazardousness and vulnerability to hazards appears to be increasing. Fatalities from natural disasters have risen dramatically over the past few decades and the rate of occurrence of technological accidents, despite lower fatality rates, has also been rising. Technological accidents also pose serious consequences for long term negative effects on health and the environment. The burden of these accidents and disasters has fallen increasingly on the world's poor who are most vulnerable to catastrophic events.

Despite this evidence, hazardousness and vulnerability are not adequately indicated by fatality or recurrence figures alone. They are also a function of limited possibilities to detect hazards. The detection of a hazard, i.e., the perception of its ability to cause personal harm, is the fundamental condition for all subsequent efforts to enhance safety and enters into the very definition of what is to count as a hazard. Without the possibility of detection, all else fails in the attempt to mitigate hazards.

A critical theory of hazards can better help us understand the problems of hazardousness and vulnerability. This theory is based on a simple premise—the terms "hazard" and "mitigation" can substitute for one another if sufficient political power is brought to bear on the process of definition.

Environments become more hazardous and individuals more vulnerable as the rate of fallible social technologies implemented to mitigate hazards rises. This is a result of (1) the complexity of these technologies, and (2) the false perception of these technologies as infallible safeguards against hazards. The latter is the unintended consequence of strategies for manipulating the language of hazards. In the following chapter, I will reexamine in a more general way some of the strategies we came across in our earlier reconstruction of the Bhopal tragedy, viz., cost-benefit analysis, strategies of non-decision, and defining hazard thresholds, among others.

Finally, the social/political definition of hazardous systems distributes overall hazardousness and vulnerability unequally to specific social classes. The poor, in virtue of their poverty and limited access to information, stand to lose disproportionately from this overall global increase in hazardousness and vulnerability. The legacy of an enlightened West—the technical fix—has harmed most those whom it most urgently sought to help.

Notes

1. Dan Kurzman's *A Killing Wind* (1987) provides the most moving and detailed portrait to date of the tragic effects the Bhopal disaster has had on the daily lives of residents of that city.

2. To say a concept is essentially contested is to claim that, while it may be empirically applicable and useful in scientific research, it nevertheless contains an "radically evaluative" component that cannot be reduced to a simple quantitative formulation. This should not be interpreted to be a defect, particularly in the social sciences where such concepts form an integral part of the various disciplines'

responsibility for social criticism. It does not prevent the operationalization of the concept, nor the verification or falsification of hypotheses in which it occurs (for a similar view regarding the concept of "power" in the social sciences, cf. Lukes, Steven. *Power: A Radical View.* London, MacMillan Press: 1974; p. 9).

3. Patrick Lagadec's book *Major Technological Risk* (1982) is the major exception to this.

4. The term "disaster" is itself difficult to define. One standard definition, not without its problems, comes from the Natural Hazard Research Group at the University of Colorado in which a disaster is any event causing more than $1 million in damage, or more than 100 people dead, or more than 100 people injured. For a good criticism of this way of defining and quantifying disasters, see Turner (1979).

5. That is, calculation of magnitude of risk depends on already existing social definitions of what is safe and hazardous in a categorical sense. Over time, these definitions change as the values a society assigns to a variety of concerns change— death, the quality of life, kinship, economic aspirations, etc. (cf. Douglas and Wildavsky 1982).

6. On the notion of "involuntary risk," cf. Chauncey Starr, "Social Benefit Versus Technological Risk: What Price is our Society Willing to Pay for Safety?" *Science* 165 (September 19, 1969): 1232–1238.

7. And for Perrow, this is as true of social organizations—which respond to emergencies less well when the rules by which they operate discourage improvisation—as it is of machines.

8. One point of White's argument was that the availability of federal monies prompted increased settlement in flood plains. As more and more persons moved into these areas, believing them now to be safe or their potential losses covered, the probabilities for major disaster also rose when flooding actually occurred that surpassed the design capabilities of existing mitigations.

9. Perrow, of course, was concerned with this phenomenon primarily as it applied to technological rather than natural hazards. But the point is essentially the same. Complex mitigations for extreme natural events also fail at a higher rate than simple mitigations.

3

FACTORS AFFECTING THE DETECTION OF HAZARDS

Safety and Culture

Why were the people of Bhopal apparently so indifferent when it came to voicing their concerns about Union Carbide's operations? Certainly, most of the residents were too involved in the daily routine of making a living and caring for their families to think much about what went on inside the plant. They assumed—and nothing really challenged this assumption—that the facility was in capable hands, and that if something were to go wrong they would receive adequate warning. After all, Union Carbide was highly respected in India. It was a technically sophisticated company. It provided many jobs and community services, and it manufactured products that would protect the region's grain harvest. If it couldn't handle its own problems, who could?

At first glance, the affinity between hazards and mitigations appears to raise questions similar to those asked in the newly emerging field of risk analysis: Given that some degree of risk characterizes most human activities, how does one decide which risks are acceptable and which are not? What can be done to protect oneself from risks which are judged to be unacceptable (or, for that matter, acceptable)? Finally, is it worth it? How much does this protection cost versus the economic and social benefits it returns?

Questions like these, however urgent it is to find answers for them, generally assume that risks are something given, even though a concerted effort must be made to "discover" and evaluate them, and that the risk analyst's job is simply to analyze the available data in order to make an informed judgment about the desirability of embarking on risky projects.

And this is true regardless of whether risks are conceived as variable states of the environment or are merely revealed through the elicitation of individual preferences (cf. Douglas and Wildavsky 1982, pp. 68–69). Changing the analytic focus from objective to so-called subjective (perceived) risk does not fundamentally alter this assumption. Preferences, no less than measured states of the environment, are the raw materials from which the academic edifice of risk analysis is constructed.

I have suggested that the awareness of a hazard depends on the possibilities for detecting it. Nothing, of course, guarantees that one will become aware of a threat simply because one has the capacity to do so. Similarly, awareness of a hazard does not in and of itself guarantee that appropriate protective actions will follow. Possibilities for making the potential for harm visible are only enhanced or diminished by the presence, type, and quality of information at one's disposal. In any case, risk, in its subjective sense, is never something "given". The perception of the potential for harm is a function, among other things, of language and the prevailing system of cultural values.

This picture, however, is incomplete as it stands. With so much talk today about risk, it is easy to forget that the world is not simply one immense hazard. Any awareness of the potential for harm implies a corresponding sense, however vague, of the potential for *safety* (or security, gain, benefit, freedom from risk, etc.)—even if only because hazards themselves serve as warning signs instructing us to exercise caution. But the relationship between perceptions of harm and safety has nothing absolute or universal about it. It is always characterized by a certain ambiguity arising from the attempt to project present conditions into an uncertain future, where it becomes increasingly difficult to separate expected gains from losses (Douglas and Wildavsky 1982, pp. 27–28). A calculated balance between expected gains and losses is always relative to a particular time and social space, to be upset as the language of hazards or the nature of the threat changes, or if an actual disaster occurs. A sense of personal safety, analogous to personal harm, depends on how one's relevant environment is defined, i.e., on a discursive, historically and culturally changing logic of hazards and mitigations.

In the literature of risk analysis, a locally achieved balance between harm and safety is often characterized as a decision problem (Fischhoff et al. 1981, p. 2; Lowrance 1976, p. 75; Kates 1977, p. 34). At any given time and relative to their circumstances, persons are faced with choices whose outcomes may either enhance or diminish their personal safety.

They examine the set of options and tradeoffs (as best they can) and decide which option from the set would be most acceptable. But again, this presupposes some prior categorical knowledge of what is hazardous and what is not. Risk analysis does not proceed in a cultural vaccuum. In one sense, the cultures into which we are born have already marked out their environment into safe and hazardous zones before a set of options can be constructed from which an acceptable choice is possible. It is only from a preexisting cultural base that a calculated assessment of the degree of risk (the relative balance between harm and safety) can be tied to a decision about the appropriateness of a particular response (e.g., how much immediate attention is required to alleviate the threat, how much we are willing to pay for protection, what kinds of regulations are needed, etc.) (cf. Kasperson 1977, pp. 54–64). To be fair, most risk analysts do not deny this, but few (with notable exceptions like Mary Douglas and Aaron Wildavsky) pursue its full implications.

The set of things defined as safe or unsafe thus varies within what can only be described as an informal culture of safety (cf. Douglas and Wildavsky 1982, pp. 1–11; Kates 1977, p. 18; Barkun 1977, p. 228; Moore 1964, p. 195).[1] Any number of items may qualify for inclusion in or exclusion from this set depending on prevailing values, beliefs, and practices. Far from exhausting the field, so-called natural and technological hazards, if they are seen to be hazards at all, form only one subset of complex and overlapping ensembles which, taken together, characterize the overall risk confronted by a particular culture (there are also such things as economic, political, and even spiritual risks—the cycles of depression/recession/unemployment, civil strife, war, taboo, magic, etc.) (cf. Kates 1977, p. 7).

This variable complexity makes it impossible to define in any absolute way what is to count as a hazard, who is vulnerable or at risk, and who is safe. Are hazards only those events which create the potential for sudden and dramatic losses of life or property? Or are they long-term processes that reveal their potential only slowly and uncertainly? Is vulnerability to hazards a function of global trends, such as overpopulation, periodic crises in capitalist production, or ecological deteriorization? Or is vulnerability a localized phenomena? Is mitigation a strictly technical issue? Or a social issue? Are risk and safety environmental, institutional, or personal concerns?

If we want to answer each of these questions affirmatively, it requires abandoning definitions of "hazard," "vulnerability," "risk," "mitigation," and "safety" that are narrowly conceived or theoretically inflexible. Because

FIGURE 3.1   An expanded model of the hazards process

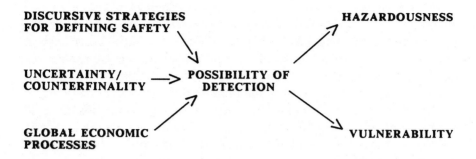

their meaning depends so much on cultural context, it is in our interest to define these terms quite generally if they are to serve any broad critical goals—hazards as potential mitigation failures; mitigations as potential hazards; vulnerability as the inability to effectively respond to hazards; and perceptions of relative harm or safety, i.e., risks, as outcomes of discursive practices (both lay and scientific "talk" regarding the nature of hazards and mitigations). With the flexibility derived from open-ended concepts, threats that are relevant only to the limited concerns of particular cultures may be considered without having to restrict the analysis to these concerns alone.

An Expanded Model of the Hazards Process

Once we move beyond the issue of harm and include the problem of safety, a whole new set of questions arises about the relations between detection, hazardousness, and vulnerability. How does safety come to be defined in the multiple discourses on hazards and mitigations, and what role does detection play in this process? What are the possible effects (both intended and unintended) of cultural practices designed to enhance safety? How is safety distributed within social class systems? Each of these questions revolve around a unique set of theoretical concerns in the social sciences which we can use as a guide to reformulate and expand the provisional model of the hazards process given in the last chapter (Fig. 3.1).

First, the question of the definition of safety emerges as a special case of the general role of discourse in forming objects of cognition and perception. In the context of the present study, an examination of the processes that enter into defining a situation will serve as a basis for identifying the symbolic and political mechanisms that affect hazard and safety awareness. Second, the question of the effects of culturally adopted safety practices emerges from general considerations in the theory of rational action. Specifically, we ask how safety practices have come to be rationalized and what the potential consequences of this rationalization process are. These consequences are examined in terms of an extended analysis of the general logic of counterfinality and uncertainty we dealt with briefly in the preceding chapters. Third, the question of the distribution of safety across social classes can be situated around a general framework describing the structure and operation of what I will call the "global hazards economy"— the international trade in hazardous technologies. Specifically, how do global economic factors, such as relations between corporations and states, set the conditions whereby detection possibilities for hazards are limited and the world's poor come to accept the risks of living in an increasingly hazardous environment?

Discursive Strategies for Defining Safety

As I noted earlier, response to hazards is conditioned by the actor's capacity to define the threat as *real*, i.e., to say that it exists and assign to it the label of potentially harmful or safe. The hypothesis that persons will take differential actions to protect their well-being based upon their linguistic means for recognizing harm or safety is one that can be drawn from W. I. Thomas' theorem that situations defined as real are real in their consequences (Thomas and Thomas 1928, p. 19).

I reiterate that the terms "hazard" and "mitigation" need not have different empirical referents. In Bhopal, the chemical facility operated by Union Carbide and each of its component subsystems was *simultaneously* a hazard and a mitigation. Most of the time, the discourse on the hazards at Carbide's pesticide plant involved debates between technocrats, the media and the public over the potential social costs and benefits of chemical production in India. Predictably, technocratic arguments stressing benefits triumphed over relatively minor public resistance emphasizing costs. The Union Carbide facility was overwhelmingly viewed as an acceptable risk rather than as an unqualified threat, a provider of jobs and savior of Indian agriculture rather than a potential poisoner of the environment.

The discourse on hazards, and the extent to which it forms objects of perception as safe or unsafe, is a special case of the cognitive and perceptual functions of symbolic communication:

The social process, as involving communication, is in a sense responsible for the appearance of new objects in the field of experience of the individual organisms implicated in that process. Symbolization constitutes objects not constituted before, objects which would not exist except for the context of social relationships wherein symbolization occurs. Language does not simply symbolize a situation or object which is already there in advance; it makes possible the existence or appearance of that situation or object, for it is part of the mechanism whereby that situation or object is created (Mead 1934, quoted in Stone et al. 1966, pp. 7–8).

Whorf (1956) has noted the implications of this social defining process for action in an example that aptly illustrates the points I am attempting to make here about safety and hazards. Because of its importance, I shall quote his remarks at length:

In the course of my professional work for a fire insurance company, . . . I undertook the task of analyzing many hundreds of reports of circumstances surrounding the start of fires, and in some cases, of explosions. My analysis was directed toward purely physical conditions, such as defective wiring, presence or lack of air spaces between metal flues and woodwork, etc., and the results were presented in these terms. Indeed it was undertaken with no thought that any other significance would or could be revealed. But in due course it became evident that not only a physical situation *qua* physics, but the meaning of that situation to people, was sometimes a factor, through the behavior of people, in the start of the fire. And this factor of meaning was clearest when it was a *linguistic meaning*, residing in the name or the linguistic description commonly applied to the situation. Thus, around a storage of what are called "gasoline drums," behavior will tend to a certain type, that is, great care will be exercised; while around a storage of what are called "empty gasoline drums," it will tend to be different—careless, with little repression of smoking or of tossing cigarette stubs about. Yet the "empty" drums are perhaps the more dangerous, since they contain explosive vapor. Physically the situation is hazardous, but the linguistic analysis according to regular analogy must employ the word "empty," which inevitably suggests lack of hazard. The word "empty" is used in two linguistic patterns: (1) as a virtual synonym for "null and void, negative, inert," (2) applied in analysis of physical situations without regard to e.g., vapor, liquid vestiges, or stray rubbish, in the container. The situation is named in one pattern (2) and the name is then "acted out" or "lived up to" in another (1), this being a general formula for the linguistic conditioning of behavior into hazardous forms (Whorf 1956, pp. 135–137).

One can agree with Whorf that hazardous forms of behavior are conditioned by linguistic meanings. Still, the connection between language, cognition/perception, and action (or inaction) is problematic; it cannot be established without overcoming the arbitrary character of the signification process itself.[2] Labeling an object is an empty gesture unless it induces persons to see and act toward the object in terms of that label. In short, labels must be persuasive and their application backed by appropriate sanctions. They gain currency through a process of *negotiation* backed by *social power* (tradition, custom, law) (Sheff 1970, p. 235; Goffman 1959). It is theoretically possible for labels to be generated by actors who have equal access to, or equal resources bearing on, the process of negotiation. It is more common, however, for labeling to be the outcome of asymmetrical power relationships. Certain actors inevitably are able to exercise more influence over the defining process—they are able to set agendas, delimit rules for discussion, and enforce decisions about the appropriate use of language (Edelman 1964, pp. 22–43; Edelman 1971, p. 7; Bachrach and Baratz 1963, p. 635; Bachrach and Baratz 1970, pp. 39–51; Lukes 1979, p. 24).

The labels that emerge from asymmetrical interactions thus have not only symbolic but also *normative* force, which means they create expectations for practical action. This raises a key question for the present analysis—who defines safety and by what license, and what effect does this have for the public's ability to detect and respond effectively to a hazard? Considered generically, safety is the concern of everyone. It is a common theme found, in myriad forms, in all cultures. Individuals make decisions regarding their personal safety every day of their lives. Concerns over safety are reflected in social practices bearing on the care exercised over one's body and the risks to which it is exposed. Concern also extends to the safety of others, both close (family, friends, neighbors) and distant (future generations). Social practices of safety are rooted deeply in the cultural histories of peoples and depend on a variety of informally developed rules-of-thumb for coming to terms not only with the environment (considered on a grand scale), but also more mundane affairs such as diet, travel, and sexuality. In the broadest sense, the social technologies of safety that exist today do so only against this background of an informal culture of safety. The latter can be conceived as a taken-for-granted set of mitigation symbols, rules and practices developed historically and reproduced by tradition.

The importance of traditional ways of dealing with the problem of safety, however, began to diminish with the rise of industrialism and urbanization in the 18th and 19th centuries. The informal culture of safety once found in every society is rapidly being replaced by increasingly formalized and rationalized means of insuring health and well-being (Barkun 1977, p. 228). Safety concerns, particularly in areas where hazards have the potential to adversely affect large numbers of people concentrated in urban environments, have today become the property of state (and state-subsidized) bureaucracies. Today, responsibility for safety is largely concentrated in the hands of government or quasi-government regulators, scientists and experts, and corporate overseers—a professional, technocratic class assigned to the task of managing our increasingly risky lives (cf. Fischhoff et al. 1981, pp. 61ff.). This technocratic class is in one sense the new bearer of the culture of safety that once existed, and continues to exist, in pre-industrial societies. In the short space of a few decades it has literally transformed long held cultural views on matters of health and disease, war, economic dislocation, natural catastrophes, production accidents, etc. To examine how safety is defined is to focus on the strategic discourse of this class.

Technocratic discourse—which ranges from scientific to overtly political—is inherently strategic, deriving from bureaucratic goals of self-augmentation and self-preservation (cf. Benveniste 1979; Ellul 1964). The political and economic stakes involved in defining and assessing potential harm and safety are high indeed in both industrialized and industrializing nations. When the assessment process fails, as it did in Bhopal, the loss in terms of legitimacy to scientists, corporations, and the state can be great. In warranting social policies that will profoundly affect the safety of large numbers of persons, technocratic discourse must balance the public demand for accountability in the event of a disaster against profitability and the maintenance of authority. In this way, technocratic discourse mirrors an arena of struggle for the control of public perceptions of safety and harm. It is a complex game whose outcomes are difficult to predict, and it is far from certain that it is only the public that feels safe that grants legitimacy to technocracy. The public that perceives chemical production facilities *as* hazards may be appeased by thoroughly researched environmental impact statements, land use (siting) regulations, social disaster insurance, or evacuation plans—costly measures but ones which nevertheless can be claimed to reduce hazardousness and vulnerability and increase public safety. But the perception of these facilities as hazards may also force a decision to halt their construction, sacrificing in the wake of this decision needed jobs, the promise of agricultural self-sufficiency, and perhaps political legitimacy. Conversely, defining chemical plants *as* mitigations against food shortages may promote their construction and thereby serve to enhance the level of public protection from this type of hazard. But perceptions of chemical facilities as mitigations may encourage public settlement in proximity to these facilities because of the employment possibilities they create, thereby reducing the safety of those who choose or are allowed to reside in these areas and, again, creating legitimation problems.

Technocrats, whose job is to define acceptable levels of hazardousness and vulnerability, are aware that certain political tradeoffs have to be made to enhance the legitimacy of their position as the cultural bearers of safety. But which ones? And what are the specific effects of these tradeoffs for hazardousness and vulnerability? Finally, who do these tradeoffs really benefit? Answers to these questions—*including the question of what exactly counts as a tradeoff*—involve the use of discursive strategies.

Of the variety of strategies open to technocrats to address these questions, four merit particular attention. We have already come across these strategies as they related to the Bhopal disaster in Chapter 1, and I now wish to reexamine them in more formal terms. They are (1) cost-benefit decisions, (2) the setting of thresholds, (3) limiting the causal chain of hazards, and (4) the strategies of non-decision. Other types of strategies are undoubtedly available. For my purposes, however, the above are particularly important because they also have the effect of limiting the possibilities of detecting hazards. Such strategies can circumscribe actions that might otherwise reduce the overall level of threat from the environment because they may induce an *unwarranted public perception of safety*. In the following sub-sections I will examine how this is possible.

Cost-Benefit Decisions

Perhaps the most common strategies that technocrats use to solve the definitional problems of hazards and mitigations are formal decision methodologies (cf. Kates 1977, p. 27; Fischhoff et al. 1981, pp. 101–105). One large class of these methodologies are the various forms of cost-benefit analysis. Simply stated, cost-benefit analysis selects from a range of technical options the one that can be shown to produce the greatest expected amount of economic benefits relative to its costs. With regard to the choice of methods to control pests, for example, cost-benefit analysis may be used to decide among organic, inorganic, biological, or environmental controls (or some particular mix of these controls) (cf. Norris 1982, p. 25). This form of analysis may also be used to decide on more specific mitigation measures within each of these alternatives. In each case, the effective outcome of the analysis is the definition of a particular technique or set of techniques as a hazard (a preponderance of costs) or a mitigation (a preponderance of benefits). The analysis itself is used to inform one about the relative degrees of hazardousness, vulnerability, safety and risk in economic terms.

Because cost-benefit analysis informs in this matter, it can itself be defined as a type of mitigation, i.e., cost-benefit analysis is a practical tool intended to enhance safety. But then, like any other mitigation, it has the potential for failure and thus the potential to increase hazardousness and vulnerability. There are several ways this can happen.

Perhaps the most serious criticism leveled against cost-benefit analysis is its inability to calculate relative harm and safety in other than economic terms. All potential consequences of a decision to implement a technical solution to a problem that are not amenable to this kind of valuation are automatically excluded (Parish 1976). But how is one to attach, other than arbitrarily, an economic value to things like the quality of human life or the aesthetic appreciation of the natural environment? In accepting only data that can be expressed in market values, significant—perhaps the most significant—hazards are hidden from view. And it is important to realize that they are hidden as a function of the analysis, i.e., as a function of the selective discourse of cost benefit research itself, which considers only those values that can be reduced to a common denominator (cf. Douglas and Wildavsky 1982, p. 71). While Carbide's operations in Bhopal could legitimately be expected to strengthen the economic base of the city and the region's agricultural export market, the potentially negative effects of such an industry on the traditional values and lifestyle of Bhopal's resident could not be calculated so easily. Because they could not be couched in the neutral language of cost-benefit analysis, these values, and the threat posed to them, were systematically, if unmaliciously, ignored. The limited framework of the model of economic choice, which devalues all arguments incapable of being set forth in its language, effectively glossed over the public discussion of these values when the time came to decide whether to license the facility. The public was persuaded that, economically at least, the decision was a good one. And, until the accident, that seemed to be sufficient.

In a related way, cost-benefit analysis may fail by being applied only to a prelimited range of alternatives. For example, if the choice of pesticide technologies is restricted to that between organic chemicals (such as the methyl isocyanate used at Bhopal) and biological controls (e.g., sterilization of male insects), the benefits resulting from a switch to (perhaps) safer environmental types of control (e.g., the release of pests' natural enemies in the environment) would be systematically excluded from cost-benefit analysis. The outcome would then be the adoption of a technology that is safest only in reference to the available alternatives. The chosen technology may, however, be quite dangerous in relation to other alternatives that were not even considered. The perception of safety which results from the *use* of cost-benefit analysis may then be quite illusory, for the *overall level* of hazardousness and vulnerability may increase depending on which elements were included in the original set from which a choice is made.

This potential failure of cost-benefit analysis is related to general problems of uncertainty that plague all formal decision strategies. No strategy of this type can possibly account for all the unintended economic effects (externalities/second order consequences) stemming from the implementation of a given technology. It may not be foreseen, for example, that the adoption of programs to alert the public of potential dangers from earthquakes may adversely affect the location of businesses in some communities (cf. Mileti et al. 1981, p. 23). Cost-benefit analyses have built-in limits for dealing with uncertainties that transform their own use into potential hazards.

Finally, all decision methodologies such as cost-benefit analysis may, because of the aura of scientific rigor that surrounds them, give the public a false sense that all important factors necessary to the analysis of a hazard have actually been taken into account (Kates 1977, p. 27). Many persons are willing to believe that if experts perform an exhaustive analysis of costs and benefits, there is little else to be done regarding the definition of hazards and mitigations. This very perception, however, may itself be a hazard in that it discourages attempts to obtain additional information relevant to the issue of safety (Slovic et al. 1974, p. 200).

Setting Thresholds

A second strategy employed by technocrats to define what is to count as a hazard or mitigation has to do with the establishment of thresholds. In contrast to cost-benefit types of analysis, which generate economic projections in order to choose from a set of pregiven alternatives, setting thresholds involves defining the *level at or beyond which a particular technology poses an unacceptable risk.* Generally, this means establishing some kind of performance safety standard (cf. Fischhoff et al. 1981, p. 1). If, for example, the threshold of risk involved in chemical pesticide production is defined as the potential release of toxic materials over a broad geographic area involving many casualties, periodic smaller releases within a manufacturing plant itself may be viewed as acceptable. Such small scale accidents may even be used as evidence that the overall system is safe, i.e., that backup mitigation devices are functioning properly to prevent potential toxic releases from crossing the predefined threshold.

In setting the threshold of risk at high enough levels. the relative perception of safety is enhanced (provided that the numerical expression of the threshold is understood in the first place). High thresholds can make hazards appear insignificant. Dams that can withstand 100 year floods invariably seem safer than structures designed to cope with 50 year floods— at least until a 100 year flood occurs. We may be more inclined to accept toxins in our food that appear to require the ingestion of huge quantities before their adverse affects might be noticed. In general, the higher the threshold of danger, the less likely are we to voice our concern, as the potential for harm literally fades from view.[3]

But the issue is more complex. Regardless of whether a threshold of risk can be determined to be high, low, or somewhere in between, the very idea that a threshold exists at all can be hazardous. Any threshold of risk may be used as an excuse for failing to implement social preparedness measures for normal mishaps that occasionally flare up below the threshold. Routine accidents that do little damage may not seem to require much attention or to justify the costs that would be necessary to avoid them, even though their effects may be cumulative or irreversible. Nevertheless, since there appears to be a direct relation between performance standards and cost, there is a marked preference, particularly within corporate enterprises, for higher thresholds. We have seen that many persons living close to Union Carbide's Bhopal facility were unprepared for the large scale accident that they were assured would never happen (Bowonder et al. 1985, pp. 6–8; Sharma and Singh 1985, p. 82). Here is a case where the perceived safety of a complex system of backup mechanisms, combined with poor social preparedness measures, defined the threshold of risk so high that when an unanticipated failure occurred the outcome was catastrophic. The defining process itself established how the hazard was to be perceived and directly contributed to the magnitude of the disaster.

FIGURE 3.2 Limiting causal chains

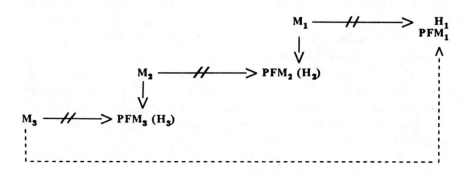

Limiting Causal Chains

A third strategy, closely related to setting thresholds, involves limiting the perception of the causal chain that has the potential to lead to disaster. Chapter 2 noted that mitigation has two possibilities—to eliminate or reduce a hazard or, through its potential for failure, to constitute a hazard of its own. Figure 3.2 gives a schematic representation of this process in terms of a causal system:

In this diagram, mitigation (M_1) eliminates the threat posed by the first order hazard (H_1). But the potential failure of M_1 poses another, second order hazard (H_2), which in turn is checked by a second order mitigation (M_2), and so on. Essentially, this is the reasoning behind the implementation of backup systems, and it is similar to the problem of thresholds—H_1 in the above diagram indicates a preset threshold.

But the causal chain of hazards, mitigations, and potential failures must end somewhere. There are two possible alternatives: first to arbitrarily cut off the linear sequence, or second, to close this sequence by forming a causal loop. In the latter case, a potential failure in M_3, i.e., PFM_3, would constitute H_1, the first order hazard (the dotted line in Fig. 3.2).

Both of these alternatives, once again, may have negative consequences for the perception of safety. By cutting off the sequence at a particular mitigation, one in effect states that nothing further can be done to safeguard against its potential failure. In essence, the hazard that is posed by the potential failure of this last order mitigation is defined away. The system appears safe, i.e., the hazards go undetected, until the time an actual failure occurs in the last order mitigation. But, in the absence of further backup mitigations, the effects of this failure have the potential to reverberate throughout the entire system, with perhaps catastrophic and irreversible results (depending on where the initial threshold of risk is set). In the Union Carbide facility at Bhopal we saw that there was a pervasive lack of backup mitigations that could have been implemented in the event of higher order failures (Bidwai 1985c). These might have included such diverse things as the installation of second order monitoring gauges on the production line or correcting existing faults in the plant's vent scrubber system.

Closing the causal loop, on the other hand, produces a different set of difficulties. By performing this step, particular mitigations are assigned multiple functions. In Figure 3.2, M_1 must be designed to safeguard against both the first order hazard *and* the potential failure of M_3 (PFM_3). But multiple function mitigations have the potential for complex interactions that may not be fully predictable and hence controllable. The interaction of mitigations may produce possibilities for failure that lay outside the capacity of the closed system to counteract. As the complexity of multiple function mitigations increases, hazardousness and vulnerability can also be expected to increase (cf. Perrow 1984, pp. 278). At Bhopal, no one fully expected the interactive failure of those multiple systems that had been established to insure the system's safety. As noted earlier, backup storage tanks designed to hold escaping chemicals were not empty, and this feature combined with failures in both the system of water spouts and a flare tower built to neutralize toxic gas leaking into the atmosphere (Bidwai 1985b). The defining processes that establish the appearance of safety of these closed systems result in systematic blind spots or points where hazards become undetectable. Again, depending on where the threshold of risk is preset, the consequences may be both catastrophic and irreversible. In the final chapter of this book, I will specifically focus on this issue in an attempt to develop some general criteria for enhancing detection possibilities in the chemical industry.

Non-decisions

Finally, technocrats (particularly politicians who depend on technical knowledge to set policy) have the marked tendency to deal with the tradeoffs involved in questions of safety by simply defining the problem away—a decision, inherently strategic, not to decide (cf. Kates 1977, p. 13). Rossi et al. (1982, p. 20) have noted that the political salience of issues regarding hazards is quite low in relation to other types of government priorities (unemployment, crime, balancing budgets, etc.). The solutions to the problems of hazardousness and vulnerability thus often appear to be blocked by a widespread political structure of "non-decisions" (Bachrach and Baratz 1970, pp 43–46). Public officials, for example, often believe that *any* gesture indicating an interest in hazards, regardless of content, is sufficient to give the appearance that something is being done to counteract the problem (Rossi et al. 1982, p. 22). In these circumstances, hazards are rendered undetectable because one has gambled that they will not become the focus of public attention in retrospect, i.e., because an actual disaster has created the political constituency that would demand effective mitigation to be undertaken. Given the rare occurrence of major disasters or accidents within any given time or locality, those who are genuinely concerned with hazards—e.g., those employed by disaster assistance or relief agencies—must often sell hazards programs to public officials who are uninterested because of the absence of a prior, effective constituency. Looking the other way from hazards because they have not yet resulted in losses of course does nothing to reduce overall hazardousness and vulnerability. But it may augment these problems, in a way resembling a self-defeating prophesy, by creating a sense of complacency, safety, or invulnerability which leads to inaction.

Political non-decisions may also increase hazardousness and vulnerability by limiting funding for mitigative technologies that would be able to detect hazards in advance, before they become actual disasters. These detection technologies, like any other mitigation, have the potential for failure and may themselves generate hazards. But the risks involved in such failures are certainly less than the risks posed by the absence of detection possibilities entirely, if solely for the reason that not all mitigations have equal potentials for failure. When basic detection possibilities are severely limited by a general atmosphere of indecisiveness, hazards are not perceived at all, or they are perceived only in retrospect after a disaster has already taken its toll. When this happens, however, the question of safety has been posed too late.

Unintended Effects of Mitigation

Habermas (1984) has noted that an essential feature of all forms of rational action is their fallibility. Failure may occur both in the process of rational communication and in the technical rationality of means-end relationships. In both cases, failure reflects the inadequacy or unreliability of our knowledge. In both cases the action does not "come off"—it produces effects that may be unintended or irrational:

> What does it mean to say that persons behave 'rationally' in a certain situation or that their expressions can count as 'rational'? Knowledge can be criticized as unreliable. The close relation between knowledge and rationality suggests that the rationality of an expression depends on the reliability of the knowledge embedded in it. Consider two paradigmatic cases: an assertion with which A in a communicative attitude expresses a belief and a goal directed intervention in the world with which B pursues a specific end. Both embody fallible knowledge; both are attempts that can go wrong. Both . . . can be criticized (Habermas 1984, p. 8).

While I have now argued at some length that traditional modes of defining and assessing safety have to a large extent been displaced by highly rationalized mitigative strategies that themselves carry newer and potentially more lethal consequences, it may still be hard for some to accept that what at first glance appears as progress toward a safer world may actually be making that world more dangerous. Mitigations are designed to reduce hazardousness and vulnerability, not increase them. When the latter occurs, the rationality of the mitigation process itself is somehow subverted (or more accurately, subverts itself). In the following subsections I reexamine in more formal terms two mechanisms that can explain how this can happen—counterfinality and uncertainty.

Counterfinality

Again, it is by way of their potential for failure that all mitigations become hazards. Although failure can take many different forms, I have been emphasizing a generic problem characteristic of all mitigations: their tendency to induce a feeling of complacency—the perception of safety that arises from believing a given mitigation will function as it was intended in the event of an emergency. I have claimed that such a perception may lead to *inaction*—inaction that may result in a catastrophe by way of a self-defeating prophesy in the event the mitigation actually does fail. But, as with everything else that relates to hazards, there are exceptions. Like Whorf's example of lighting a cigarette near gasoline drums marked "empty," thinking we are safe can also lead to concrete *actions* that at first appear to be eminently rational but only serve to intensify the level of danger.

There are many examples to illustrate how our belief in the rational efficacy of mitigation can make us do things which, quite literally, backfire in our faces. Some of these examples have already been given but are important enough to restate here.

Relief supplies of food are certainly a mitigation for people living in regions stricken by drought, and undoubtedly save many lives. But if too much relief is sent (i.e., if too many nations act as suppliers), the result may be bottlenecks in distribution, economic disruption, or long term dependence of populations on outside help (which may dry up as quickly as it materialized, redoubling the problem). The content of aid, while both rational and well-intentioned, may be totally inappropriate, as Wijkman and Timberlake (1984) note with a touch of black humor:

> Stories abound in the relief field of completely inappropriate aid: the British charity that sent packs of tea, tissues and Tampax; the European Community sending powdered milk into an earthquake area where few cows had perished, but there was no water; and the West German charity which constructed 1,000 polystyrene igloos which proved too hot to live in. But the igloos could not be dismantled or moved. They had to be burned down, and when burning gave off toxic fumes. Tins of chicken cooked in pork fat have been sent to Moslem countries which do not eat pork. Blankets donated to India were donated by India to Nepal, which donated them back to India; the blankets were never needed or used. Turkey after a 1983 earthquake asked donors not to send any medicine or second-hand clothes, but a Northern donor flew in a few days later with a planeload of precisely these items—and a TV crew to cover the distribution (Wijkman and Timberlake 1984, p. 108).

When everyone becomes involved in the relief game, the collective effect may be counterproductive. Similar processes are at work in other forms of mitigation. If, when given a warning, everybody tries to evacuate a location at once, the result may be that no one can get out in time (the classic example is yelling "fire" in a crowded theater). A warning siren that is repeatedly tested only at 12 p.m. on Sundays will be useless for a disaster that strikes at 12 p.m. on Sunday.

These examples illustrate the operation of *counterfinality*. Counterfinality occurs when a set of actions, each of which are (or at least appear) rational in the individual case, produce unintended and disvalued effects for the aggregate (Elster 1978, pp. 106–122).

Perhaps the best known illustration of counterfinality in sociological theory derives from Marx's explanation for the falling rate of profit in capitalist societies (Marx 1967, Chapters XIII–XIV). Individual capitalists, seeking to increase their profits, mechanize their operations in an effort to reduce wage costs. But if all capitalists behave in this manner (which is rational for the individual capitalist), the outcome is an increase in unemployment and a lessening of the overall system's capacity to extract surplus value. The result is a decline rather than a rise in the rate of profit. Individual rationality produces collective irrationality.

In the literature on hazards, examples of the operation of counterfinality are far from rare, although not always explicitly recognized as such. Several authors have noted the desensitizing effect resulting from too many disaster warnings which prove to be unfounded (Anderson 1969; Mack and Baker 1961, pp. 6–7; Breznitz 1984, pp. 11–16). When a real warning comes, no one believes it. To take another example provided earlier, the clearing of forests in Third World countries, rational for the individual or corporate landowner seeking to increase available land for agriculture or raise profits, poses a greater threat of flooding for the collective (Wijkman and Timberlake 1984, pp. 57–62). Similarly, pesticide use, rational for the individual farmer at one point in time, may produce long-term problems resulting from the development of resistant strains of insects, or "super pests" (Norris 1982, pp. 19–25). General hazards, such as those arising from the overexploitation of resources, pollution, and rapid population growth also exhibit features of counterfinality (Elster 1978, p. 110).

Counterfinal outcomes for individual mitigative efforts rest on several assumptions (taken either singly or in combination): (1) that not everyone will behave in the same fashion at the same time, (2) that not all mitigative systems will fail simultaneously, and (3) that the actions of relevant others at time t_1 will be roughly the same at time t_2. If each individual acts on one or more of these (supposedly rational) assumptions, the mitigative actions that ensue may be collectively irrational, i.e., they may produce the opposite of their individually intended results. For example, action on the first assumption—that not everyone will do the same thing simultaneously—may result in the aforementioned incapacity of states to deal with overabundant relief coming from a variety of well-intentioned donors. Similarly, assuming that not all safety systems may fail simultaneously may lead to a failure to consider the interactive effects of some mitigative technologies. Perrow (1984, Chap. 1) provides an example of this with regard to the failure at Three Mile Island where no one believed that isolated multiple function mitigations could generate an entire system failure. Finally, action on the third assumption—that actors will behave similarly between time t_1 and time t_2—overlooks effects such as the "cry wolf" syndrome noted above. Potential victims (including those who issue warnings) may become desensitized to repeated false warnings.

Uncertainty

Potential failures in mitigation systems may arise not only from rational assumptions about the behavior of others or the improbability of certain events, but also from the inability to form *any expectations whatsoever* regarding the outcomes of mitigation (in itself a kind of undetectability of hazards). In the latter case it is common to speak not of counterfinality but of radical uncertainty in the selection and implementation process itself.

Simon (1959) has noted that classical decision analysis, which presupposes rational choice by actors regarding pregiven alternatives with known outcomes, is inadequate as a model for explaining how decisions are actually made:

> The classical theory is a theory of a man choosing among fixed and known alternatives, to each of which is attached known consequences. But when perception and cognition intervene between the decision-maker and his objective environment, this model no longer proves adequate. We need a description of the choice process that recognizes that alternatives are not given but must be sought; and a description that takes into account the arduous task of determining what consequences will follow on each alternative (Simon 1959, p. 253).

With regard to the selection and implementation of mitigations, uncertainties can for simplicity be grouped into two broad categories—those involving the physical parameters of an environmental extreme, and those dealing with social outcomes of the extreme event (Bogard 1986). Uncertainties regarding the former include such factors as the time of occurrence (Graham et al. 1983, p. 7), the magnitude of the event (Saarinen et al. 1984, p. 75; Moore 1964, p. 87; Savage et al. 1984, pp. 122–128; Sorenson and Gersmehl 1980, p. 27), the proximity of the threat (Diggory 1956), and the recognition of the event itself (Anderson 1969; Erikson 1976, p.

20; Perry et al., p. vi). Uncertainties regarding social outcomes include the possibility of panic (Savage et al. 1984, p. 124; Scanlon et al. 1976, p. 42; Quarantelli 1974, Introduction), pressure from outside groups (Sorenson and Gersmehl 1980, p. 129; Gray 1981, p. 359), evacuation problems (Greene et al. 1981), role ambiguity and conflict (Perry and Mushkatel 1984, Chap. 1; Erikson 1976, p. 20), and many more (cf. Mileti et al. 1985). With each type of uncertainty the possibilities for the detection of the hazard involved is limited.

Uncertainty generally arises from difficulties in obtaining or processing information (Turner 1979, p. 55). One way these difficulties may increase a mitigation's potential for failure is by altering the timing of its implementation. For example, problems in obtaining or processing information may delay the notification of relevant authorities, the latter's notification of the public, or the decision to evacuate hazardous areas (Mileti et al. 1981, pp. 93–96). A warning or evacuation order issued too late may actually be worse than no warning being given at all, especially if it is hastily worded, conveys the uncertainty of officials, or generates confusion.

To return to the example of foreign assistance, relief supplies often arrive too late to substantially aid disaster victims. Wijkman and Timberlake (1984) have noted that the most pressing needs of victims are usually within 48 hours of a disaster. Information processing difficulties, however— often political in nature but also those generated by the disaster itself— can cause delays. Aid arriving after this time can often interfere with victims' own attempts at recovery:

> Human nature dictates that when a plane arrives with free goods, people will stop what they are doing and queue for hours to get whatever is available, whether they need it or not. Thus relief can actually slow down reconstruction and interfere with self-help (Wijkman and Timberlake 1984, p. 110).

Conversely, uncertainty may force mitigation to be implemented too early. Premature warnings may be forgotten, ignored, or unwisely acted on if a disaster does not materialize within a reasonably expected time frame. In Bhopal, there were at least two individuals who warned residents of the dangers of the Union Carbide plant years in advance, but as time went on with few accidents these warnings lost their salience (Bowonder et al. 1985, p. 8; Bhandari 1985, p. 104). The same process also works for natural hazards. Much of the debate concerning the issuing of warnings for earthquakes is based on the wide time frames that may separate the warning and the actual event. Action on warnings of this type may produce clearly unintended effects. Mileti et al. (1981, p. 23) have speculated that such warnings have the potential for economic dislocations in the communities in which they are issued. Corporate enterprises may be dissuaded from locating in areas that have been declared earthquake zones, this despite the fact of the tremendous uncertainties in pinpointing the precise time, location, or magnitude of the forecast event.

Finally, uncertainty can be a function of the complexity of mitigation itself. Difficulties in obtaining or processing information are exacerbated by mitigations that are tightly coupled and interactive. When multiple function mitigations are involved, it becomes increasingly difficult (and takes increasing amounts of time) to pinpoint the exact location of particular mitigation failures. In extreme cases the result may be catastrophic. It can be argued, for example, that the complexity of the system designed to detect an incoming nuclear attack is so great that a false warning may not be corrected in time to halt a decision for a "retaliatory" strike. Here the potential failure of the system negates any possible benefits that could derive from its implementation. Detection of the hazard (which in this case is the system of mitigations itself) has become impossible within the time frame in which a decision must be made.

Global Economy, Hazards, and the Poor

Up to this point, my concern has been to sort out some rather general mechanisms—definition strategies, uncertainty, and counterfinality—through which the possibility of detection of hazards decreases and the potential for harm increases. I now want to tie these reflections to my other major concern, viz., the rising vulnerability of the world's poor.

With regard to natural disasters, we have seen that the poorest countries have the highest mortality rates per disaster. The poor probably suffer higher casualties in the wake of major technological accidents also, although we must await more detailed studies before making such a generalization. Still, other things being equal, it seems less likely that a Bhopal-like tragedy could happen as readily in a country like the United States. But why should this be true?

One answer immediately comes to mind: resources. The United States (and wealthier countries in general) have the material and political resources available for implementing complex and elaborate mitigation schemes to safeguard against technological (and natural) disasters, whereas poor nations do not. I do not believe, however, that this argument (along with its implicit assumption about how to solve the problem of differential vulnerability) is totally adequate as it stands. I have suggested that technocratic strategies— particularly those that result in the adoption of complex technologies, but also those whose effect is to increase absolute levels of mitigation itself— may heighten overall hazardousness and vulnerability, at least over the long run. By this argument, wealthier nations too may be setting themselves up for future disasters with potentially large scale consequences. This is mainly because the plethora of complex mitigation mechanisms available to these countries has tended to push the thresholds of risk ever higher. When these thresholds are crossed, i.e., when a given system of mitigations fails, the results are increasingly likely to be devastating. There is already some evidence that property losses from disasters have dramatically risen in wealthier countries over the last several decades (cf. Burton et al. 1978, p. 14). In the long run, it is possible that the higher potential for failure of complex mitigations may increase fatality rates in high income countries also, despite the obvious difficulties in trying to establish this proposition.

Thus, the argument to intensify mitigation efforts in poorer nations so they are modeled on those of wealthier ones is not an adequate answer to the problem of differential vulnerability. It certainly cannot be an unqualified answer. In reality, this answer conceals a class logic that lies at the foundation of the discourse on hazards and mitigations. Specifically, we must ask what (if any) social class benefits from the authority to decide among mitigation alternatives, establish thresholds, limit causal chains, and make non-decisions. And what social class is harmed by this authority?

It was suggested above that for technological and natural hazards, the primary locus for mitigation decisions lies with technocrats. But technocrats are also concerned with hazards of a much more general nature—production shortages and oversupplies, threats to economic self-sufficiency, and so on (recall the distinction between general and specific hazards in Chapter 2). It is often the case that decisions dealing with technological hazards are contained within and referred to these larger concerns, which often provide the ideological justification for the introduction of these hazards (cf. O'Connor 1973, pp. 101–116). In Bhopal, for example, the government license to Union Carbide of India to build a plant in which methyl isocyanate (MIC) was to be manufactured was based on the belief that the chemical industry would provide needed jobs and capital (Bowonder et al. 1985, pp. 7–8; Engler 1985). Methyl isocyanate, it will be recalled, is also used to produce pesticides that control insects and increase food production— the central focus of India's U.S. imposed "Green Revolution."

Hazards are thus sometimes portrayed by technocrats as having their origins in universal human needs and desires—or "demands" in economic terms (cf. Bowonder et al. 1985, p. 9). In the effort to satisfy these demands (for food, energy, security, etc.), and to produce profits for enterprises established to meet such demands, hazardous technologies are introduced into the environment. These in turn require mitigation.

Human demands, however, are not the source of the problem—except in the most abstract (re: ideological) sense, they vary from society to society and over time. A more radical interpretation of technological hazards would inquire into the *production* of such demands in the first place within the context of functional prerequisites of political and economic *systems*. Such an interpretation is first and foremost rooted in a consideration of the global economy.

Global Economic Pressures— the World-System, Hazards, and the Poor

To understand the relation between the production of demand and the implementation of hazardous technologies, it is necessary to digress briefly to outline the general logic of this relation.

The central argument is that the historical development of the capitalist world-system has organized interstate production relations, both politically and economically, in ways that promote both an increasing marginalization of weaker states and a corresponding dominance and centrality of strong states. One result of this development, as I shall argue below, has been the tendency to transfer hazardous production technologies from states in the "core" (primarily Northern Europe, the U.S., and Japan) to states in the "periphery" (the economically depressed and politically weak nations that comprise the so-called "Third World").

Hopkins (1979, pp. 23–24) has characterized theories of the development of the capitalist world-system in three ways. First, there is one expanding world economy that has taken a variety of contingent historical forms in the relations between states. This world economy has a single, or "axial," division and integration of labor processes paralleled by a single set of accumulation processes between an historically advanced and geographically shifting "core" and an historically retarded, enlarging, and geographically shifting "periphery." The terms "core" and "periphery" are themselves primarily world-economic categories and reflect, albeit roughly, the similar but not fully equivalent distinction between rich and poor states (keeping in mind that rich and poor are also categories that apply to *intra-state* populations). In the capitalist world-system, such economic distinctions tend to coincide with political consolidations—strong states, in relation to others, tend to form in core areas; weak or marginal states develop or are developed in peripheral areas. In the theory of global economy, it is important to remember that "peripheral" does not mean marginal in the sense of dispensable. Core states *need* peripheral states for their development. Without both cores *and* peripheries, there is no capitalist world development (Hopkins 1979, p. 25).

Second, there are expanding multiple states that, through economic competition and political rivalry, continually form and terminate in the inter-state system. Alliances and coalitions take place between and among states in regular attempts to extend their dominance in relations to one another. Such processes lie at the center of both imperial and anti-imperial movements.

Third, and importantly, there is a world-system relation between labor and capital, which is both produced by and a condition of the process of accumulation on an ever expanding scale. This relation is the context that organizes, in specific and contingent historical forms, inter-state production (supply) and consumption (demand) relations, and inter-state politics. In the latter, formally rational-economic considerations governing the accumulation process come to replace substantively rational considerations (in Marxist terms, exchange value increasingly dominates use value). In the relation between cores and peripheries, economic exchange becomes increasingly unequal and leads to the "underdevelopment" and poverty that characterizes the periphery (Wallerstein 1979, p. 73).

The model of the accumulation process, initially propounded in its most comprehensive form by Marx in *Capital*, Part VIII, is perhaps the key to understanding the development of the world-system. It has been the starting point for subsequent theoretical reflections on the global economy culminating in the works of Baran, Wallerstein, and others over the last 25 years.

Wallerstein (1982, Chap. 1) has argued that the central motive of entrepreneurs in core economies is accumulation (or alternately, the self-expansion of capital), considered as an end in itself rather than a means for increased consumption. When the accumulation process is blocked, entrepreneurs seek ways in which to overcome periodic economic crises, or bottlenecks, that derive from surplus production (cf. Baran 1957, pp. 22ff.).

For Wallerstein, the contemporary world system of states creates conditions where accumulation can freely flourish. In the past, states have traditionally stood in the way of ceaseless accumulation because of their legitimate interest in the appropriation and redistribution of wealth, i.e., states have historically placed limits on entrepreneurial activity. But modern states do not, and cannot, contain economies. Rather, for Wallerstein, it is the fact of a single global economy that contains multiple states in competition that has created free reign for the process of accumulation. Competition among states promotes internal pressures for them to control their work forces and to give monopoly advantages to accumulators (Wallerstein 1982, p. 13). The competition among states has allowed the pace of technological change to increase rapidly in the global economy. But increasing the rate of change of technology (and the increasing rationality that this appears to imply) has resulted in the aforementioned polarization of the global economy into cores and peripheries along with the polarization of class structures both within and between states.

Within the modern world economy, demand for goods is no longer a function of production of commodities per se, but of the way the wealth produced by entrepreneurial enterprises is distributed to owners and workers. But because of the desire of individual states for economic stability, demand tends to remain fairly stable over the middle run while the supply of goods tends to ever higher levels (overproduction) (Baran 1957). This process generates periodic crises or bottlenecks to accumulation.

These crises call for solutions that, on one side, take the form of seeking new markets (the creation of demand), introducing new products, or reducing production costs. On another side they call for action to change patterns in the distribution of wealth, a source of the anti-imperialist movements that have dominated political struggles in the post World War II period (Wallerstein 1982, p. 19; Amin 1982, pp. 190ff.; Baran 1957). Both solutions require practical "adjustments" in the location of activities of production (primarily from cores to peripheries) and in wage and salary levels (primarily reductions) (cf. Hopkins 1979, pp. 30–35; Bluestone and Harrison 1982, pp. 42–46).

Hazardousness, Vulnerability, and Global Economics

How does the model of the capitalist world-system relate to the increase in hazardousness and vulnerability and their redistribution to the world's poor (who reside primarily in the periphery)? First, within core countries hazardous production technologies have come under increasing state regulations (cf. Bluestone and Harrison 1982, p. 17; Norris 1982, pp. 28–30). These regulations drive up both the political and economic costs of production and produce falling rates of profit, with the effect of mounting pressure to relocate these technologies (controlled by multinational corporations) to states on the periphery (where costs are less because regulation is less). Alternately, the intense competition between states both creates and promotes, i.e., in effect *defines*, the demand for technology transfers. This is reflected in the core ideology of growth and accumulation that parallels and justifies the introduction of hazardous production enterprises in the world-system. The states making up the periphery, in their desire to modernize, often see in these technologies the promise of economic benefits and the reduction of political pressures stemming from poverty and population problems.

If we put this in the terminology developed in Chapter 2, a hazard (this time at the most general level of a whole productive technology) is cognitively transformed into a mitigation through an ideological discourse that legitimates the competition of multinational corporate enterprises for capital. The influx of these enterprises into peripheral states often attracts large masses of the poor to production sites in search of work. In Bhopal the population nearly doubled in the five year period that followed the construction of the Union Carbide facility (Bowonder et al. 1985, p. 7). These people, primarily poor, in turn suffered greatly from the lack of more specific mitigations that may have protected them from an accidental release of chemicals from the facility, a lack that probably would not have been tolerated in the United States. These demands—for higher wages and better jobs, for economic stability and self-sufficiency that the use of chemical pesticides promised—created the pressure for the introduction of a hazardous technology. But these demands are also shaped by formal functional imperatives of the global economy.

The ideological structure of the global economy also has implications for losses suffered from natural disasters. The correlation between intensive production, ecological deterioration, population clustering, and the resulting losses from natural disasters (floods, hurricanes, drought) is heightened in states on the periphery (Wijkman and Timberlake 1985, Chap. 1). Again, advantage is taken of peripheral states' eagerness for capital and the lack or under-enforcement of state regulations that would mitigate against the indiscriminate use of resources. The intensive use of technology and losses from natural disasters are not independent phenomena. Again I note how rapid deforestation in the Third World has promoted more frequent and intense flooding and vulnerability to storm surges, the major causes of death from disaster in poor countries (Wijkman and Timberlake 1985, pp. 53–57). Intensive agricultural practices (designed to move poor nations from subsistence to export economies) may also have this effect where programs are lacking for the reclamation of valuable topsoils.

Underlying the operation of global economic factors, one again finds the operation of social defining processes where the discursive transformations of hazards into mitigations are at work to enhance the feeling of safety. In general these are as follows:

First, at the level of decision methodologies, a problem emerges when all the alternative mitigations among which decision-makers must choose are technologically complex. Complex mitigations might, however, be singularly inappropriate for developing nations that lack the resources to manage them (cf. Lovins 1979, p. 3). Possible failures of these technologies have a greater potential to generate losses in countries poorly equipped, both economically and politically, to bear the costs of developing specific mitigations (warning systems, relief measures, evacuations and the like) (Bidwai 1985, pp. 63–69). Nevertheless, the implementation of high risk, complex technologies seems likely to continue, both as a result of global economic pressures to expand markets and reduce production costs and the perception of many nations in the periphery that complex technologies alone promote rapid economic growth and political stability.

Second, core and peripheral states are likely to establish different thresholds of risk. In the core states these thresholds are likely to be higher (have less potential for catastrophic failure) (Norris 1982, p. 11). Regulations in these states are more likely to control the introduction of technologies with very low thresholds of risk (this despite attempts by some enterprises to alter perceptions of these technologies to make them appear to have higher thresholds). In contrast, states on the periphery are less likely to resist the development of low threshold technologies (Dehli Science Forum Team 1985, pp. 206–210). Again, the promise these technologies hold for economic and political stability are probably dominant motives for this, although pressure for adoption from enterprises in core countries is undoubtedly a factor.

Third, core states are likely to have more restrictions that prohibit the cutting off of causal hazards' chains at points where further mitigations could conceivably be implemented (although at higher costs) (cf. Norris 1982, pp. 13–19). Training levels of hazardous production workers, for example, is often higher in core states along with the use of extensive redundancy equipment to back up fallible systems (Bidwai 1985c). In view of global economic demands to cut costs, peripheral states are unlikely to be able to implement or enforce such stringent requirements.

Fourth, attempts to introduce mitigation policies into political agendas, or to prohibit the introduction of certain technologies altogether, are more likely to fail in poor countries (Ramaseshan 1985, pp. 95–101). This is due in part to the pressing economic problems in these states and their consequences for stability (which take priority), and in part to the difficulties of the poor in gaining access to their own political systems. The structure of non-decisions with regard to hazards in the periphery is likely to be more rigid than in wealthier countries (Ramaseshan 1985).

Fifth, relocation of hazard/mitigation technologies to peripheral countries effectively reduces the problems of counterfinality and uncertainty associated with these technologies in core countries. The intended effects of counterfinality and uncertainty are often (although not always) localized phenomena, i.e., negative effects are generally relegated to specific geographical regions. But counterfinality—collectively irrational outcomes generated by individually rational actions—differs from the effects of uncertainty in that for the former actors and victims form overlapping groups (Elster 1978, p. 109). The Indian people's decision to accept pesticide production at Bhopal was based on the rational assumption that this would mitigate some of the negative effects of a rapidly growing population (cf. Bowonder et al. 1985, p. 7). But construction of the facility was in part responsible for some of the intense uncontrolled migration into Bhopal and the areas surrounding the plant, contributing to the high number of casualties when the accident occurred.

Uncertainty—lack of information regarding all possible outcomes of action—in contrast produces negative effects of externality, i.e., actors and victims may form separate groups. By relocating productive technologies to peripheral areas, core nations transfer the hazard potential associated with these technologies to underdeveloped regions that are often ill-prepared to cope with externalities. In the global economy uncertainty—in the form of unforseen bottlenecks to accumulation—is a prime motive for the relocation of these technologies.

Conclusion

In this chapter, I have attempted to link the general problem of discursive hazard/mitigation transformations to three general theoretical concerns: the social definition of the situation, unintended consequences of rational action, and the structure of the global economy as the development of a capitalist world-system. With regard to these respective orientations, the following points relevant to a critical approach to hazards emerged:

First, the transformation of hazards into mitigations and mitigations into hazards is accomplished through at least four general discursive strategies: (1) decision methods, most notably cost-benefit forms of analysis, (2) the setting of thresholds of risk, (3) limiting causal chains, and (4) non-decisions. Each of these strategies itself constitutes a particular mitigation oriented to the problem of safety. Each, therefore, has a potential to fail (notably by limiting possibilities for detecting hazards) and to produce negative consequences for hazardousness and vulnerability.

Second, the discursive transformations of hazards and mitigations are rational actions that may generate unintended effects. Transformations occur within contexts of uncertainty that include difficulties in obtaining or processing information that is used as a basis for decisions regarding hazardousness. An integral feature of these difficulties is the complexity of mitigation systems. Counterfinality occurs when the rational action of individuals—based on inadequate assumptions about the behavior of others or the concatenation of events—produces negative outcomes for the collective.

Third, the structure of the global economy in terms of the development of a capitalist world-system creates conditions for (1) the increasing polarization of states into cores and peripheries having unequal capacities to deal with hazards, and (2) the transfer of hazardous technologies to the periphery where recurring disasters produce disproportionately greater losses. Global economic processes are linked with symbolic transformation processes to alter the possibilities for detecting hazards. This is particularly true for transformations that change the perception that certain technologies may have catastrophic potentials to the perception that these technologies are mitigations safeguarding economic and political stability.

Notes

1. The concept of an informal culture of safety owes much to Moore's (1964) idea of a "disaster culture." I cannot go into his idea in any detail here, except to say my notion of a culture of safety is in many ways the reverse compliment of Moore's conception. While Moore noted that communities having past experience with disasters were culturally better prepared to deal with emergencies, his concern did not really extend to the question of why people feel safe, which to my mind is crucial to account for what happened in Bhopal.

2. On the arbitrary character of linguistic signs, cf. Ferdinand de Saussure, *Course in General Linguistics*. La Salle, Illinois: Open Court Publishers, 1986; pp. 100ff.

3. Although, like all questions involving risks, there are important exceptions. The risk of being hijacked by terrorists on a flight to the Middle East is infinitely smaller than the risk one takes each time s/he sits behind the wheel of an automobile. Still, most Americans have second thoughts about flying to Islamic countries, but rarely think twice about the risk of being involved in a fatal car crash. Once again, it is not so much a question of the objective risk each action involves, but of the cultural and symbolic frameworks within which risks are perceived, and the political or economic ends for which these perceptions are manipulated.

4

CONCLUSION AND
RECOMMENDATIONS

No More Bhopals?

What can be learned from the Bhopal tragedy? Can similar crises be prevented from erupting in the future? Even though history tells us that the chance for another industrial accident of comparable magnitude is relatively small, it would be doing an injustice to potential victims of technological disasters to view Bhopal simply as an isolated incident whose probability of recurrence elsewhere was negligible. We must resist uncritically embracing the old maxim that the exception proves the rule, i.e., that the Bhopal tragedy was only a "freak" accident, a statistical anomaly to comfort us with the thought that if it does happen again it will be a long time coming. Rather, the fact that Bhopal came as a complete surprise should only increase our sense of unease about modern chemical technologies. Even more, it should make us wary of statistics which tell us that disaster is unlikely. The unlikelihood of a major disaster should not, like it did for the victims of Bhopal, make us feel complacent.

Maybe instead we should see Bhopal as a "normal" accident, symptomatic of a trend in industrial production toward routine technical failures with ever higher potentials for catastrophe. But while this has the advantage of shaking us out of our complacency and sharpening our critical eye, it also marks our unsettling sense of powerlessness over the outcomes of our own technical creations. If and when such accidents have reached the deplorable point of becoming routine—a function of complexity outpacing human control—what can be done short of "pulling the plug" on the machine itself? But for those technologies that have already become so ingrained in our everyday lives that we find it difficult to imagine living without them, hasn't this become a utopian dream?

Statistics and probabilities—the staple diet of the modern discourse on hazards—inevitably fall short when it comes to finding answers for what are essentially moral, political and cultural questions. Nevertheless, it is impossible to get very far in a search for a way out of the complex problems posed by modern technology without some recourse to the arguments they support. Despite many misgivings, I am forced to admit that, in its more critical moments, the contemporary analysis of technological risk has something important to say. One problem is getting industry and state bureaucrats to listen. The other, far more difficult, is getting them to inform the public about the dangers to which it is exposed.

In the following pages, I will offer some provisional conclusions regarding the vulnerability of the poor to chemical production accidents of the kind for which today the Bhopal tragedy serves as a global symbol—of the best humanitarian intentions gone sour, of sacrificing safety for profit, and of technical rationality working against the public good. I will examine several criteria—uncertainty, irreversibility, catastrophic potential, and dependency—against which assessments of these technologies can be made to decrease the chance an accident like the one in Bhopal will repeat itself. These criteria are not infallible—to think otherwise would go against everything I have argued for in this book. Nor are they new. In fact, with the exception of dependency, they have all been recommended before in the risk literature. Yet because enforcement of their use as standards of assessment has the potential to severely retard the pace of industrial development (and, if applied consistently and rigorously, even bring it to a standstill), they have met with strong corporate and state resistance. They are rarely given the serious consideration they deserve when set against short run concerns of profitability, economic growth, political expediency, and so forth.

I am not suggesting that these criteria be used exclusively by industry (or state agencies) to make their own decisions about which technologies are acceptable and which are not. Rather, they are intended primarily to sensitize residents who are forced by circumstance to live in proximity to chemical plants to the worst possible consequences that might befall them. They are offered with the suggestion that such residents (and all concerned citizens) should demand their unconditional use in any decision to implement a given technology. In the final analysis, however, this decision must rest with the public itself. In saying this, I reject numerous arguments which claim the public is too naive or technically unsophisticated to evaluate risk information or to know the difference between low and high probability worst outcomes.[1] Although public overestimation of certain risks is a well-noted phenomenon, no study, as far as I am aware, has demonstrated either convincingly or conclusively that the long-term dangers of overestimating risk are any greater than leaving technical decisions solely in the hands of industry or state "experts."

Uncertainty, irreversibility, catastrophic potential and dependency must first be recognized for their value as benchmarks in making choices about whether to adopt certain technologies, and only secondarily as taken-for-granted conditions of implementation. No one, of course, can predict or control every potentially hazardous outcome associated with a given technology. But this fact does not have an exclusively negative significance. The simple knowledge that uncertainties, irreversibilities, etc., are possible in a general sense is an important consideration when it comes to making decisions. In developing these criteria, past experience with the pesticides industry, like past experience with disasters in general, provides only one key to the problem. Nevertheless, we shall have to address this issue by looking critically at the past safety record of the chemical industry. Overall, this record ranges from marginal to good, but this should not blind us to the tremendous potential of this industry to cause harm to health and the environment.

For all its horrors, the disaster in Bhopal had at least one beneficial consequence. The intense public debate that followed the gas leak sensitized more private citizens than ever before to significant but previously unrecognized hazards in the chemical industry as a whole. Still, no chemical accident is exactly the same. If another tragedy like Bhopal occurs, it is highly unlikely to manifest the same chain of causal factors or to produce the same types of outcome. For this reason, the criteria to be examined below are important for mandating that as many *worst-case scenarios* as possible be taken into consideration and presented publicly to all potentially affected parties before the industry is allowed to move forward. For one thing, this means no more advertising or marketing campaigns designed to convince the public of what a great advantage it would be to have a chemical plant in their community. Enhanced detection of hazards can only mean that even the least likely accidents have to be considered.

My approach is to emphasize caution and does not call for the immediate and unconditional elimination of the pesticides industry—at least not yet. The Bhopal tragedy understandably makes us want to pull the plug on the machine, but first we must consider often compelling arguments to the effect that elimination of this industry may cause more problems for poor countries than it solves. It would be unwise to dismantle a whole industry if the consequences of such an action decreases agricultural output, jeopardizes jobs, or in effect re-places these countries in the intolerable position they were originally in before the introduction of hazardous pesticides.

Hazardousness and Vulnerability in Bhopal

It is hardly surprising that the Bhopal tragedy cost the poor most dearly. Bhopal is one of the poorest cities in India (Diamond 1985c). The city itself has grown swiftly since it was designated the capital of Madhya Pradesh in 1956. As we have seen, some of this growth can be traced to the modernization efforts that opened the doors for industries like Union Carbide to locate there in the first place (Bowonder et al. 1985, p. 7). In Bhopal, there are few conveniences that are commonplace realities for the populations of more industrialized nations. There is only one telephone per 1,000 people, and running water is a luxury. The city itself is intensely crowded, and people share living space with cows, goats, horse-drawn carriages, cars and bicycles. Everywhere there is the stark contrast between old and new, rich and poor. Industries like Union Carbide's facility and the attractive homes of plant managers and government officials stand out distinctly in a 2,000 year old city steeped in both a rich tradition and squalid living conditions for the poor (cf. *New York Times* 1985e). It is hardly surprising that Western technology has appeared as an attractive solution to the many problems that face cities like Bhopal and India in general.

We have seen how the events leading up to the Bhopal accident involved incredibly complex system and component failures, errors in judgment, overreliance on market mechanisms, wrongheaded definitions, misinformation, lax enforcement of regulations, and wishful thinking. At every point in the system of mitigations a counterfactual question could be posed: if this potential failure could have been averted, could the tragedy have been avoided? Even as the debate rages on, the question itself appears increasingly sterile, especially if it is directed at lower level hazards. Neither simple technical improvements (more gauges, better warning systems and worker training, etc.) nor refinements of local regulatory policy could have postponed the accident indefinitely. Bhopal was too caught up, like many cities of the Third World, in a vicious cycle of hazards that is coextensive with the entire framework of modern industrial development.

I have argued that one common feature united the system of failures, errors in judgment, regulatory laxness, etc., and that was their impact on the public detection of the hazards at Bhopal. How did a hazardous production facility and process like Carbide's come to be seen as safe, necessary and beneficial? And how did this perception directly affect the hazardousness of living in Bhopal and the disproportionate vulnerability of that city's poor? Let us briefly review some of the details.

As I noted earlier, very few individuals—either victims or experts—foresaw or believed in the potential for an accident of the magnitude that occurred there. But even if the accident clearly caught most people by surprise, there were some prior indications of safety problems at Bhopal. The significance of these early warning signs was muted by several factors: the reluctance of the company to become involved in the day to day affairs of the plant's safety and maintenance routines (despite the control it exercised over budgetary and other high level decisions), the costs of new equipment and training, and the dependence of the region's farmers on pesticides (a dependence itself generated by new agricultural methods and technologies introduced from the West). From the very start in Bhopal, possibilities for detection became increasingly constricted by the economic and political expediencies of producing chemicals for consumption by the Third World. At the lowest level of the socio-economic ladder, the possibilities for detection had all but been eliminated. The slum-dwellers living near the plant took their safety for granted. Most had no idea what was being manufactured at the plant; those who did had no idea of its toxicity. They heard no warning (or rather, were unable to distinguish between real and practice warnings), nor did they have the resources to communicate a warning to others (by telephone, through the press prior to the event, or to their representatives). Plant workers had only the bare minimum of emergency equipment and virtually no knowledge about how to handle non-routine events (Diamond 1985c).

Without these basic capabilities, the general climate of misinformation and non-information only added to the poor's already high vulnerability. The vast majority of those severely affected by the gas leak were already living in near starvation conditions. Many of them suffered from various forms of respiratory diseases and health problems associated with overwork and malnutrition, and routine pollution from industries in the area—not least from Carbide's plant itself—certainly didn't help matters (Report of the Dehli Science Forum Team 1985, p. 195). In the confusion that ensued during the tragedy and not knowing where to turn, many of the victims ran directly into the clouds of escaping gas. They did not have access to modes of transportation out of the area that were available to wealthier citizens. Even the buses that had been purchased by Union Carbide to aid in evacuation in the event of an emergency were not used— plant workers were too concerned with saving their own lives during the leak to pay much attention to them (*New York Times* 1985a). Medical treatment of the victims at Hamadia hospital, ironically supported by Union Carbide funds, was slow, uncertain, and severely hampered by the massive number of casualties.

Finally, we have seen that most of the poor in the slums around the plant had no real choice about where they could live. They supported themselves in whatever fashion they could, and would have fared even worse if forced to move. Recognizing this, city officials allowed them to stay, but also did nothing to relocate the plant itself. Nothing seemed to be able to shake the status quo prior to the accident, and in the general atmosphere of non-decisions a certain resignation and trust in others to define their personal safety became instilled in the future victims of the disaster (Diamond 1985b; *New York Times* 1985b).

Could the poor's vulnerability have been reduced had they known about the hazards of MIC, the immediate dangers surrounding its production, or the possible long-term effects of the chemical when released into the environment? While I have no doubt that this would have been the case, in asking this question I am not assuming that the ultimate cause of the accident was the lack of detection. I have already rejected the idea that such ultimate causes can be given for disasters. In any case, the *absence* of a mechanism logically cannot serve as a cause. Further, as I noted in earlier chapters, detection does not in itself guarantee that effective action of any sort will follow. Other resources (communication, transportation, etc.), had they been available, could arguably have reduced vulnerability. The crucial issue here, once again, is that when detection fails, so does every other possibility of mitigation. It is in this sense that detection forms the ground for subsequent mitigation efforts. It cannot be asserted that in Bhopal no one detected the hazard. But the tragedy is focused around the fact that the poor had the *least* possibilities for detection and that without these possibilities even the simplest actions for protection or avoidance were unknown to them.

It doesn't take much imagination to see that limited possibilities for detecting hazards is a problem for the poor in all areas of the Third World, and not just where the potential for a sudden and dramatic catastrophe is high. Many end users of pesticides in the Third World, notably poor farmers, have difficulties reading or understanding warning labels on chemical containers or have not been trained in their safe handling and method of application. The result, as we have seen, are many deaths annually. Most of these deaths occur in India, a country that, ironically, is most supportive of Western pesticides technology to ease its food supply problems. If the Bhopal tragedy teaches anything, it is that these technologies do not automatically fit the cultural traditions and ingrained habits of persons living in Third World nations (they have their own specific cultures of safety), and that general mitigative policies to relieve the pressures these nations face often have counterfinal outcomes. The line between hazards and mitigations often becomes blurred in seductive images of economic growth and self-sufficiency.

Therefore, it was not the *impossibility* of detection that led to the increased vulnerability of the poor in Bhopal. It was the fact that the *possibilities* for the detection of hazards that were present in a vague and unorganized manner from the very beginning were systematically eliminated. Political tradeoffs to enhance legitimacy and global economic demands generated by the capitalist imperative of accumulation narrowed the chances for detecting the dangers at Bhopal. The hazards associated with pesticides production came increasingly to be seen as mitigations against more general kinds of hazards—food shortages, unemployment, the pressures of population growth, and economic dependency. In the attempt to mitigate against these hazards, specific short-term risks were introduced into the socioeconomic environment of Bhopal and thereby increased the hazardousness of living in that city.

But even the use of the concept "short-term risk" to characterize potential outcomes is misleading and increases the chance of limiting detection possibilities. Concentration on immediate outcomes loses sight of the fact that perhaps a quarter of a million inhabitants of Bhopal face possible *long-term* health complications from their exposure to MIC (Bowonder et al. 1985, p. 12). And the Bhopal tragedy itself forms only one small story of the global trade in pesticides—it is difficult to predict the extended implications of continued reliance on chemical pesticides for the people of all nations or for the natural environment. The picture of hazardousness that emerges from this reliance is not comforting. It is thus not immediately apparent that improving the possibilities of detection by specific measures (better warning, more training, etc.) for those living and working in immediate proximity to chemical production facilities constitutes anything approaching a satisfactory answer to the problems of hazardousness and vulnerability to chemicals in general. Undoubtedly, adequate instrumentation, technical training, early warning and better preparedness plans all would have contributed to saving lives in Bhopal. But such measures do not even begin to address the *general* problems involved in the production of pesticides.

As long as the global network of pesticide manufacturing and consumption continues to be perceived as necessary, beneficial, and safe, a fundamental detection mechanism ultimately fails. The inability to detect and plan for long-term hazards, whether because of genuine uncertainties, the desire for profit, or a blind faith in our good intentions for the poor of the Third World, virtually insures that accidents like the one at Bhopal will not be the last. If a tragedy like Bhopal does not repeat itself, a probability that is unlikely given increasing reliance on complex, interdependent technologies, the continuing export of untested and unregulated chemicals from core countries poses an increasing risk of environmental degradation. Even the growth in employment opportunities which runs parallel to the expansion of the industry is problematic. Every year in the Third World the rate of increase in worker poisonings from low-level exposure to pesticides keeps pace with the rate of increase in imports from the West (Norris 1982, p. 23). These processes, however, occur so slowly—like the movement of a glacier—that they have little effect on ingrained perceptions of safety or the acquired need for these chemicals. The use and production of chemical pesticides in the Third World has, unfortunately, become little more than a "calculated risk."

The development of specific mitigation measures therefore cannot begin to address the problem of the global increase in hazardousness resulting from chemical production. Worse, it can make persons feel safer in their own communities while the dangers continue to mount all around them. This is exactly what happened in Bhopal, even in spite of the fact that many things should have been done to protect the lives and health of Bhopal residents from the leak that occurred on December 2, 1984. In the Bhopal tragedy, the existing system of mitigations was perceived to be adequate. Merely increasing the number of specific mitigations cannot guarantee such a tragedy will not occur again. Indeed, it may only increase the potential for this to happen by making the existing system of mitigations more complex. To insure against a repetition of the Bhopal tragedy requires questions directed at the most general level—questions regarding the need for chemical pesticides and the global system of production and trade that pressure for their use in the first place.

The Safety Record of the Chemical Industry

Such questions must be built upon a foundation. We need to have some idea of just how safe the chemical industry is in relation to other technologies. In direct comparison to other forms of hazardous industry, the production of chemicals appears on the surface to be marginally safe. Relatively few plant operatives have lost their lives in chemical facilities— only one chemical worker died in an accident in the United States between 1980 and 1984 (Sorenson 1986). Similarly, before the major gas leak in Bhopal, only one employee death could be attributed to UCIL's operations there.

In all, until the Bhopal disaster, probably fewer than 2,000 fatalities associated with major chemical-related accidents have been recorded since 1921. The Bhopal tragedy, of course, casts new doubt on the reassurances provided by these figures. Still, the number of innocent bystanders being killed is on the increase, partly because chemical production plants have become larger, more complex, and increasingly crowded in by growing urban environments (cf. Perrow 1984, p. 120–122). Chemical production, like other modern technologies such as nuclear power, have become more highly coupled and dependent upon non-linear interactive chains, and hence more prone to "system" accidents (Perrow 1984, p. 345). But even despite the comparatively low fatality rates associated with this industry, the long-term effects of chemicals on future generations and the natural environment are virtually unknown. Pesticide end-products, as we have noted, find their way into the world's oceans, accumulate in tissue, and can return to exporting countries in foodstuffs imported from the very countries where they were "dumped" (Norris 1982, Chap. 2; Rele 1985).

These problems are causes for the utmost concern, for they point to uncertainties, irreversibilities, and catastrophic potentials that are masked by the empirical evidence of low fatality rates for plant operatives, and the comparatively low, although increasing, rates for innocent bystanders. When viewed in the long-term and linked to general policy concerns such as food production or economic and political stability, however, the causal links become blurred and risk assessment difficult. At issue is no longer actual fatalities stemming from a few major chemical disasters but rather the *potential* for such disasters to happen, i.e., hazardousness and vulnerability.

Perrow (1984, p. 120) notes how disguised these long range problems may be. Chemical facilities are familiar sights to almost everyone. They have been around for over 100 years and, except in rare incidents like Bhopal, have done very little dramatic or direct damage. Yet even some industry personnel are themselves concerned about the rapid increases in the scale and complexity of chemical plants, and the proximity of urban communities that have grown up around them in the last 15 years. Perrow (p. 120), remarkably, argues that increasing safety has accompanied this growth. In the wake of precautions taken after the first major chemical disaster in 1921 in Oppau, Germany, which killed over 500 persons, it appeared that this may have been the case. The Bhopal tragedy combined with the increasing rate of smaller scale lethal accidents over the last decade has, however, given far less reason for such optimism. Of all the major industrial disasters in the 20th century from 1921, 60% have occurred since 1975. Not all of these have produced great numbers of casualties, but the rate of occurrence itself has been alarming.

Perrow's state concern is not so much with innocent bystanders or future generations as it is with the nature of "system" accidents themselves. In drawing the boundary of concern in this way, however, his analysis stops far short of conclusions that could be drawn from including in this system long range effects, global pressures and policies, and the politics of detection. Perrow places chemical production in a category of acceptable risk because the catastrophic potential of the industry appears to be relatively low and the cost of alternatives high (cf. Perrow 1984, p. 349). But while the past record of the chemical industry appears to be marginally good in terms of safety, the issues of hazardousness and vulnerability cannot be adequately addressed by simple extrapolations from past performance balanced against economic feasibility. Perrow's employment of catastrophic potential and cost of alternatives as policy guides tends to treat these categories as givens rather than problematic (i.e., relative to cultural values and subject to negotiation). Hazardousness and vulnerability can be clarified only with additional information regarding the *future* (and not only past or present) potential for catastrophe, the possible irreversibility of consequences, and the increasing world-wide dependence on chemicals. All these issues are subject to intense debate—they form a multiple and shifting discourse on hazards. The issues raised by this discourse are clouded by numerous uncertainties that must be balanced against the short-term successes of the industry. In limiting his analysis to so-called "normal accidents"—accidents which do not cross system parameters but which nevertheless have routine catastrophic potential built into the system—Perrow is unable to assign much weight to worst-case scenarios that may conceivably transcend the bounds of the system, affecting future generations and the long-term viability of the sociophysical environment. In utilizing exclusively historical data and structural descriptions of system complexity and interdependency to ground his concept of "normalcy" for system accidents, Perrow clearly underestimates the dangers involved when living in a hazardous environment becomes increasingly more routine.

It is a big step to use the "normal" quality of accidents as criterion for recommending that a hazardous production process be accepted or abandoned. It seems preferable, at least on critical grounds, that policy recommendations for hazardous industries continue to be based on an assumption that increasing hazards are still in a very real sense "abnormal," i.e., that they can exceed system boundaries and be judged as unacceptable when they do.[2] This, I believe, can only be done by drawing the hazards system as large as possible, taking into account as many potential long range negative consequences as we can. Only in seeing hazards as abnormal events can full weight be given to the aforementioned criteria for judging them—uncertainty, irreversibility, catastrophic potential, and dependency. There is a hidden danger in seeing the Bhopal tragedy as a "normal accident." While normal accidents may be deplorable, against Perrow we need to make these accidents "stand out" and lose their appearance of routineness. I will briefly explore the preceding criteria in what follows to argue that the current system of chemical pesticide production and trade is unacceptable as it stands and must be made the subject of intense public scrutiny if we are to insure that a tragedy like Bhopal will never repeat itself. The issues, in the final analysis, do not limit themselves to Bhopal or the Third World in general. They concern all of us and our future.

Criteria for Enhancing Detection and Reducing Hazardousness and Vulnerability

Three of these general assessment criteria—uncertainty, irreversibility, and catastrophic potential—have been referred to on a number of occasions in the literature on risk, technology assessment or economic choice (cf. Kates 1977; Elster 1984; Perrow 1984; Douglas and Wildavsky 1982; Luce and Raiffa 1957; Goodwin 1978; Henry 1974; Diamond and Rotschild 1978; Arrow and Hurwicz 1972). At least one, however—dependency— I have not found specifically addressed in the literature in a way that relates to the problem of introducing technological hazards into the environment. The following pages therefore take the form of a brief review of current thinking in decision theory. The general point to remember is that these criteria do not simply signify *outcomes or conditions* of the hazards process itself but are rather to be considered as explicit guidelines for the choice of hazardous technologies. This, however, requires a crucial caveat. *Insofar as these criteria function as guidelines by which to assess hazard potentials, they are themselves forms of mitigation.* This means that they can fail and generate hazardous conditions themselves.[3] Above all we must avoid the temptation of thinking that such criteria are strictly for the use of experts and that once experts have applied these criteria we are safe. Just the opposite should in fact be the case. These are guidelines that *all* potentially affected persons should and must be made aware of. They should fundamentally alert us—general public and experts alike—to the fact that we are *not* safe from the risks posed by hazardous technologies, and that any choice of technology carries with it possible worst case scenarios that we must take into account in any implementation decision. The public has a right to know precisely what these worst case scenarios are and participate in all decisions that directly or indirectly affect their future health and well-being. In many cases, we must accept the fact that the result of employing such criteria may be a decision to forego the implementation of a hazardous technology altogether.

Uncertainty as a Decision Criterion

Uncertainty, as we have seen, is a lack of information needed to determine the probable outcomes of an action or to order these outcomes by the magnitude of their effects (cf. Elster 1983, Appendix 1). As an inherent condition of all decision-making, uncertainty limits the possibility for detecting negative as well as positive consequences of hazardous production techniques. We know from reports following the Bhopal accident that uncertainty extended even to basic research on the toxicity and appropriate methods of treatment for exposure to methyl isocyanate itself. But MIC production is only a small part of this picture. In its 1979 report, the

General Accounting Office revealed that Food and Drug Administration analytical methods had not been able to establish tolerances—allowable residue levels—for over 170 different pesticides. Even more disturbing, FDA testers cannot assure consumers in the United States that imported food is free of some 130 commonly used pesticides for which tolerances have not been set (Norris 1982). The full extent of pesticide poisoning at the global level is simply not known. The methodology for detecting tolerances is either non-existent or poorly developed and does not allow reliable inference, despite the fact that short-term data indicate the possibility of increasing dangers. So Western countries continue to manufacture and export greater amounts of pesticides believing until proven otherwise that their benefits outweigh their negative consequences, basing this belief on a rather naive hope that in the long run their efforts will be vindicated. Scientific uncertainty, rather than being accepted as a constraint on production, is transformed in the marketing process into an asset based upon information that is quite simply not available. Because it is surrounded by uncertainty, pesticide production can more easily assume the character of an acceptable risk. Perversely, the corporate attitude seems to be that the less we know, the more chances we can take.

While uncertainty as a condition limits the ability to detect hazards, and while this limitation can provide a justification for expanding the production and export of untested chemicals, uncertainty as a decision criterion has just the opposite effect, mandating that every conceivable outcome be given consideration. In the Bhopal accident, it is still not clear whether worst-case scenarios for chemical-related accidents were ever developed by the Carbide corporation specifically for its operations in India. Certainly, if they were considered, such scenarios were never made available to the residents of the city nor, from all indications, to plant employees. But this is exactly the type of information required for the public to plan for the widest possible set of negative outcomes. Instead of informing residents and operatives that their very lives would be at stake in the event of an emergency, Union Carbide and its affiliate continued to advertise the safety of the Bhopal facility, its modern technology, and, above all, the growth of India's economy and agricultural export market resulting from increased pesticide consumption. But, to put the matter bluntly, Union Carbide had no more certain information on these latter outcomes than any other type of outcome, disastrous or not. In any case, simply stating, either before or after an accident, that things can go wrong doesn't help. One cannot use the argument that things don't always work out the way they were planned as a cover for projections of future goods that, from a scientific or theoretical standpoint, one has no right to make. From a critical orientation, uncertainty must be routinely employed to make worst-case projections (Elster 1983). Only from such a list of possible negative outcomes can a "least-worst" course of action be chosen (which may mean choosing to forego that course of action). As we have seen from Bhopal, limiting or ignoring worst cases can induce the sense of complacency that compounds the likelihood of an accident.

In general, uncertainties are more likely to affect the poor than the middle and upper classes. In core countries, the chemical industry, even after years of strict regulation, still manages to produce a certain amount of skepticism and wariness among consumers. While individuals in wealthier nations may not have a real choice in what foods they eat or in determining overall production levels of chemicals, they at least have an awareness of the dangers, and that is some basis for demanding more stringent regulation or for changing lifestyles to reduce the level of risk. In poor countries, changing lifestyles is difficult at best, and Western-style regulations enacted there often fail to produce their intended effects. In 1978, the U.S. Congress moved to establish some controls on pesticide exports under the Federal Insecticide, Fungicide, and Rodenticide Act (FIFRA). This included strict rules on labeling pesticide containers to warn of possible toxic effects from misuse. But labels do little good if they can't be read or are nullified by corporate efforts to build trust or minimize the public perception of danger. From the Bhopal accident, we have seen that such trust was readily forthcoming if ultimately misplaced. In view of the real potential for harm, it is all the more incredible that the American chemical industry is nervous that the FIFRA regulations increase the likelihood that foreign governments will become more aware of the regulatory status of certain pesticides in the U.S. and possibly stop importing their products. In 1981, the National Agricultural Chemicals Association proposed amendments to FIFRA that would prohibit communications between the EPA and foreign officials concerning the export of pesticides banned at home (Norris 1982). The domestic chemical industry clearly wishes to minimize the worst case scenarios associated with chemical exports to the Third World and maintain the perceived mitigative or beneficial aspects of this export. This attitude cannot be justified on any scientific, theoretical, or, indeed, moral grounds.

If worst-case scenarios should be used in making decisions about hazardous production technologies, it must be asked whether any of these scenarios are bad enough to call for a total ban on pesticide production and export. Here the issue becomes even more controversial, especially in view of limited evidence that pesticides have contributed to increased food supplies in developing countries. Again there is a danger of equating so-called normal accidents in these countries—or at home for that matter—with acceptability. Here difficult decisions must be made balancing the long range toxicity of pesticides with a potential loss of agricultural viability and its effects on nutrition in poor countries. To address such questions means to face squarely issues of the irreversibility of outcomes to humans and the natural environment from pesticide use, the catastrophic potential of an increasingly complex and coupled industry, and the growing dependence—real or manufactured—of our lifestyles on chemical technologies.

Irreversibility

The criterion of irreversibility refers both to decisions regarding the implementation of hazardous technologies and to the consequences of those technologies themselves (Elster 1983). The technologies of pest control in agricultural development are, like most scientifically based technologies of production, in a continual state of change. While uncertainty dictates that the details of these changes can be neither predicted nor fully controlled, it is possible to take account of the general fact that techniques *will* change, e.g., that alternatives to present chemically based pesticide technologies that are safer and less environmentally disruptive may become available in the future. This is to some extent already taking place with the development of new biological and environmental methods of pest control (Norris 1982, p. 22; Mojumder 1985, p. 146). The irreversibility criterion stipulates that decisions regarding the implementation of chemical controls, whose long range hazardous consequences remain uncertain, be postponed until further information regarding safer alternatives is forthcoming. In other words, it is perhaps better to adopt a "wait and see" attitude regarding the possibility of better technologies than to make a decision to implement a present technology that may turn out in the future to be irreversible.

It is evident that the use of chemical pesticides in Third World countries like India have had some marginal effects on overall production of foodstuffs (Farmer 1977). It is also evident that alternatives were available. Even disregarding the use of biological and environmental techniques for pest control, it was noted above that less hazardous techniques for synthesizing methyl isocyanate (not dependent on phosgene or chlorine reaction) were already in use in West German chemical facilities. Despite this information, the MIC-technology available from Union Carbide was the one eventually chosen for the Bhopal plant. The end-product of both the U.S. and West German companies was of course MIC and equally hazardous. But the decision to opt for Union Carbide's technology was not delayed until more thorough research could have been done on the West German alternative, leading one to suspect that profitability and prestige were dominant motives. In the final analysis, once the production license to Union Carbide was granted by the Indian government, the decision would have been difficult to reverse. It became impossible as the plant was built and people started to move into the area.

The situation becomes more complex when biological alternatives for pest control are considered. Here research is still developing and largely unconsolidated, and it is by no means certain that biological controls would be as effective in producing added crop yields as chemical pesticides. Nonetheless, it could have been assumed that such information would have been forthcoming sometime in the future. It could be argued that if this future information were negative, i.e., if biological controls were eventually shown to be largely ineffective in increasing crop yields, not too much would have been lost by postponing the decision to opt for the MIC technology. A decision of postponement can generally be reversed. If on the other hand, later information about biological pest controls suggested it to be a safer and equally effective alternative to chemical controls like MIC, it would have been better not to make the latter decision which, once taken, becomes difficult to reverse (cf. Henry 1974).

Irreversibilities regarding the consequences of hazardous technologies to the sociophysical environment can be either strong or weak (Elster 1983, Appendix 1). Operationalizing these terms requires an argument based on thresholds of hazardousness similar to that developed earlier. Thresholds, it will be recalled, are established limits beyond which the safety of hazards systems becomes compromised and the possibility of disastrous consequences unacceptably enhanced. The manipulation of thresholds is a key factor in the detection of hazards and the interpretation of their relative safety. When uncertainty is introduced in the system, however, and when information on thresholds becomes limited or unavailable, the problem of strong and weak irreversibilities arises. According to Elster (1983, p. 206), strong irreversibility obtains if (1) one can only know where the threshold is by hitting it, and (2) it is impossible to back away from the threshold when it is hit. Weak irreversibility obtains when condition (2) is satisfied but not condition (1). The first condition is a very strong uncertainty criterion, saying we are not only unaware of how far we can go in the implementation of a hazardous technology, but that we will remain so until we have already gone too far. If we consider only the accident at Bhopal and its relatively contained effects on residents and the surrounding natural environment, the condition of weak irreversibility probably holds (although not for the *residents* of Bhopal). From the information now becoming available from the tragedy, it is probably safe to say that future mitigations—improvements in early warning, preparedness, industry siting, land use, and the like— would substantially reduce the chances for a repetition of a similar tragedy occurring elsewhere. When viewed at the level of the global system of pesticide production and export and possible long range effects on health and the natural environment, however, the situation becomes extremely uncertain and one cannot readily dismiss the possibility of strong irreversibility. Pesticide poisoning of the natural environment may be expanding at a rate that has the potential for global catastrophic consequences. It is extremely difficult for scientists to know if or when global tolerances for chemical pesticides will be crossed and result in ecocatastrophe. From the information coming in from the Bhopal tragedy, there is little evidence that strong irreversibility was ever a criterion in the decision to produce MIC. Corporate realities and India's pressing need to increase food supplies and generate economic stability appear to have successfully redefined the problem.

Catastrophic Potential

Clearly linked to the problem of strong irreversibility is the probability of catastrophic potential in the pesticides industry. In judging the acceptability of a hazardous industry, catastrophic potential is a difficult criterion to define. Perrow (1984, p. 343) defines a "catastrophe" as an accident that results in the death of over 100 second party victims, mainly suppliers and users of the hazardous system. For third and fourth party victims, i.e., innocent bystanders or future generations, Perrow's formulation is somewhat vague:

> For third and fourth party victims the most catastrophic systems are estimated to be nuclear power plants, weapons systems, and DNA accidents; all of these could be very, very large indeed. Somewhat further behind are chemical plants (largely vapor cloud explosions and release of such toxins as chlorine gas). . . . Chemical plant . . . accidents would involve third and

fourth party victims, but in the hundreds, normally, rather than the thousands or millions (Perrow 1984, p. 343).

For Perrow, the chemical industry has a "middle range" catastrophic potential. Because of this moderate potential, combined with the high cost of developing alternatives for this industry, Perrow recommends that chemical production be tolerated and improved in terms of its safety rather than abandoned (cf. Perrow 1984, p. 349). The latter recommendation he makes for technologies such as nuclear power and nuclear weapons systems, which have both high catastrophic potential and lower cost alternatives.

Perrow makes the mistake once again, I believe, of drawing conclusions about the chemical *industry* on the basis of a notion of catastrophic potential primarily applicable to chemical *facilities* (cf. Chap. 2). An accident like Bhopal may indeed appear moderate when compared to possible fatalities or injuries resulting from other more hazardous technologies (nuclear power, for example). But it is a long step from this to say that the catastrophic potential of the chemical *industry* is substantially less than the nuclear *industry*. In the early pages of my analysis, I attempted to draw attention not only to organizational and design flaws in the Bhopal facility itself, but to place those flaws within a wider system context of global pressures, uncertainties and defining processes. That is, I wished to begin specifically with the overall production system itself to explain how an accident like Bhopal could happen rather than use an accident like Bhopal to explain the catastrophic potential of the overall system. The former is admittedly not Perrow's concern—chemical system accidents are for him confined mainly to production facilities—but I believe it limits his analysis and the recommendations he can make.

To make evaluations of the pesticides industry that would benefit the public at large requires that explicit attention be focused on the uncertainties of broad social and environmental consequences from the very outset, rather than have such evaluations derived from the accident performance of a limited number of hazardous facilities. According to Norris (1982, Chap. 2) these uncertainties relate to worst-case scenarios involving threats to the global survival system. Among these threats are irreversible environmental damage and the evolution of what are called "super pests." In terms of environmental damage, the long range effects of methyl isocyanate are unknown. The past record with the indiscriminate use of other forms of pesticides, such as DDT, do not provide much comfort. Unlike MIC, the effects of DDT even seemed fairly innocuous at first. It is not acutely toxic to humans except at fairly high doses, and it is not readily absorbed through the skin. But over time, DDT use proved dangerous enough to merit calling these effects catastrophic. Used in a worldwide program to control malaria, DDT has been implicated in declining populations of waterfowl and ocean life,and laboratory tests have convinced scientists of DDT's link to cancer (Carson 1962).

In contrast to DDT, methyl isocyanate is extremely toxic at low dosage rates. But like DDT there is widespread concern about possible long ranger after-effects of MIC on different environments. In the air, MIC will undergo degradation due to sunlight, as well as reaction with moisture. The likely major products are methylamine, dimethyl urea and other gases. In soil and water, methylamine will be the major product. It will be held tenaciously by soil particles until complete degradation. In plants, MIC may compete with carbon dioxide in photosynthetic processes. In both plants and animals methylamine would be the major metabolite. Some research has suggested that these metabolites are likely to participate in complex pathologies leading to kidney disease and failure (Kumar and Mukerjee 1985, p. 133). Once exposed to MIC, any further mild exposures could be fatal (Menon 1985, p. 135).

While low toxicity rates may have been responsible for the relative lack of concern over DDT's long range effects in the early years of its use, the absence of basic research into the long-term effects of MIC given its highly toxic nature is puzzling, although not totally surprising. For once again, uncertainty, irreversibility, and catastrophic potential were never explicitly employed as criteria for the decision to produce MIC in the first place. Rather the proliferation of new industrial chemicals such as MIC reflects industry and government's constant search for one that is both profitable and appears to meet the needs created by food shortages and the desire for economic self-sufficiency. Overall long-term uncertainties are ignored because attention to such uncertainties requires postponement of decisions that would address these needs.

The problem is compounded by the fact that in the chemical industry's war against pests that threaten the food supply, the pests may be winning. Many insects have short generation times, and some produce more than one generation per year. When a pesticide kills all but the resistant individuals in a population of insects, the survivors quickly produce new generations that show increasingly greater proportions of these resistant strains (U.S. Environment Programme 1979). Norris (1982, pp. 22–23) notes that the first approach of the chemical industry to the problem of pesticide resistant strains was the development and successive application of ever new synthetic chemical pesticides. But this resulted in strains developing that were resistant to not just one but many pesticides. These so-called "super pests" have had devastating economic and health effects in countries all over the world. Thanks to DDT, for example, Sri Lanka once had as few as 23 cases of malaria in a whole year, but is now experiencing 2 million cases a year, about the same level as before DDT was ever used (ibid.). And, because of resistant strains of pests, levels of foodstuff production in India have not come near meeting the optimistic numbers that were projected at the beginning of the Green Revolution (Chambers et al. 1977).

Multiple resistance is not the only danger of using different pesticides in succession to control increasingly resistant strains. Pests may also become cross-resistant, using their acquired resistance to protect them against pesticides to which they have never been exposed or which have not even been developed Norris (1982). All this is a long way from the accident that happened at Bhopal, but it points to a key factor in determining at a global level why an accident like Bhopal occurred in the first place. Pest resistance has developed through the overuse of pesticides, but the increasing proliferation of resistant pests has in turn required the increasing use of more and different pesticides at an ever expanding rate. To break this vicious cycle means becoming aware—detection at its most basic level— of the uncertainties, irreversibilities, and catastrophic potential of this cycle and utilizing these as basic and public criteria for the decision to allow plants such as the one in Bhopal to be built. All these criteria suggest a far more cautious approach to pesticide production than has been evident in the past. One must face squarely the problem that in producing hazardous pesticide technologies we have become dependent upon them and that this dependence has resulted in disasters like the one experienced in Bhopal. It is to this final criterion that I now turn.

Dependency and the Detection of Hazards

Once a system of production and consumption like the chemical industry is established and operating for a number of years, it becomes increasingly difficult to picture a mode of life without it. Dismantling the system appears to imply a return to the very conditions that called it forth. It is argued that eliminating pesticide use in the Third World means eliminating all the benefits of the Green Revolution and a return to the devastating cycles of malnutrition and famine that have plagued those regions of the world for years. Similarly, it is argued that dismantling the pesticides industry means the loss of jobs and markets so needed by these countries to raise their standards of living. These are arguments that rage around the issue of technology transfers from core to peripheral states, and not only in the pesticides industry. When an accident like Bhopal occurs, the populations of the Third World are often double losers. They are disproportionately affected by losses from the accidents themselves and, in the subsequent pressure to close down facilities, many lose their jobs and sole means of livelihood (*New York Times* 1985e; Shrivastava 1987).

As we have seen, dependence on chemicals in the Third World is tightly connected to the development of productive but fragile new strains of seed introduced at the beginning of the Green Revolution. These strains required new methods of irrigation, farmer organization, and, of course, pest control. But as pests demonstrated a remarkable tendency to develop greater resistance to available chemicals, and alternatives to existing imported pesticide technologies were not readily available, harvests became increasingly dependent on the rapid development and application of new synthetic compounds. The introduction of biological and environmental methods of control has gone some way to reduce this dependence on chemicals, but the adoption of these methods is not widespread. Scientists are uncertain about their relative efficiency in protecting crops or their long-term environmental consequences. Another problem is that use of these techniques requires that all parties involved—government officials, agriculture and health workers, private distributors of pest control products, and farmers—have a fairly extensive understanding of ecosystems, the role of pests and predators, and the ability to coordinate a complex number of efforts (Norris 1982, p. 26). Such knowledge and expertise may be difficult to come by in the Third World—it is difficult even in the U.S.—and dependence on increasing application of pesticides continues, often with disastrous results.

Like uncertainty, irreversibility, and catastrophic potential, dependence enhances rather than detracts from the ability to detect hazards when it is transformed from a condition of implementation into a criterion for decision-making. The question of dependency is always the same: will we be able to back away from the use of a hazardous technology without regenerating the conditions that the technology was originally designed to avert? The honest reply is that the answer to this question is simply unknown at the time the technology is introduced. But it is precisely because this information is unknown or uncertain that the possibility for dependence be included in the decision to introduce a potentially hazardous technology from the outset. Only by including dependency as a possible scenario in the set of outcomes for the technology, and by informing the public of this possibility, can one legitimately take steps to elaborate alternatives should such dependency develop. These alternatives in turn should explicitly address the problem of how a given technology can be dismantled without catastrophic consequences or returning to the conditions that existed prior to the introduction of the technology. Until we have better answers to these problems, it is difficult to justify moving forward.

In Bhopal, and in India in general, no information was forthcoming to the effect that chemical production might generate dependency on the part of farmers in their agricultural practices, workers in their jobs and means of support, or the government in its development of agricultural policies. Not surprisingly, information about dependency (or any other of the criteria in this chapter) is not the kind of thing corporations trying to make a profit like to give out to the public who consume their product. But it is precisely this kind of information the public needs to sensitize them to the hazards of chemical pesticide production, i.e., that allows them to detect a hazard, however remote, at the most basic level and plan accordingly. This is not to say that information must tell *what* uncertainties, irreversibilities, catastrophic potentials, or dependencies will develop. No one can do this. What is needed rather is a systematic presentation of as many worst-case scenarios as imagination and past experience can suggest. Granted that this is a pessimistic approach to the problem of introducing new technologies, but it is the only one that makes sense given the level of hazards involved. If the people of Bhopal and Madhya Pradesh had been informed of such possibilities, if they had not been constantly bombarded with only information regarding pesticides' beneficial effects, wiser choices may have been made.

All of this is not intended to recommend the elimination of the pesticides industry—at least not yet. Given current economic and political realities, such a recommendation would most likely go nowhere, as much as I might like to argue for it. In any case, there are strong reasons backing the claim that halting the production of pesticides would cause more harm than good. These arguments must be addressed. Trying to overcome the dependence on chemicals—the Third World's and our own—involves reversing past decisions wherever possible and generating new options with less potential for catastrophe. These actions are themselves laced through with uncertainty. Nevertheless, what we should learn from Bhopal is to slow down, to back off from the quick fix and spend more time—a great deal more time—looking for and developing safer alternatives. This is what full public input would accomplish, and why it is so strongly resisted by the industry. Lastly, Third World governments should not feel so eager, or receive so much pressure, to adopt Western technologies that are themselves unregulated or considered dangerous.

Above all, focusing on the uncertainties, irreversibilities, catastrophic potentials, and dependencies created by the use of pesticides places the burden of proof for their adoption squarely on the shoulders of the chemical industry itself. It is this industry's responsibility, above and beyond making profits and reducing costs, to present the worst that can happen to the public so the latter can make informed choices. It seems that only after this is done should the chemical industry be permitted to stress its past performance record, the sophistication of its technology, or its role in the modernization of agriculture. If only the people of Bhopal had an idea of the dangers they were creating for themselves when Union Carbide was licensed to build its plant there, i.e., if only they had the basic tools for detecting the hazard, there may never have been a Bhopal—persons would not have been allowed to live outside the plant's gates, staff and training levels would not have been cut back and alternatives to MIC would have been more thoroughly investigated. Perhaps the plant would not have been built at all. We have to live with the Bhopal tragedy, but we do not have to allow another. The choices will be very difficult, however. Following Perrow, the future does not look optimistic for no more Bhopals—our technologies are too complex and too tightly coupled. But we can use Perrow's pessimism as grounds for a new start, fully aware that the dangers have once more become detectable.

Conclusion

I have argued for the conclusion that hazardousness and vulnerability in Bhopal were the inevitable outcome of limiting the possibilities for the detection of chemical hazards. By defining problems with chemical production away, by submitting to global economic pressures for chemical manufacturing, and by letting uncertainties take over to produce counterfinal outcomes, the appearance of safety in Bhopal was enhanced while the reality of the hazard went unnoticed. When the disaster struck, the residents of Bhopal were "victims" in every sense of that term. Poor to begin with, their poverty exposed them to many needless risks that in turn were downplayed by an overly optimistic portrayal of the place of chemical production in the Third World. The tragedy in Bhopal was not a "calculated risk." The loss of life on such a grand scale is not a risk at all. It is simply a state of affairs that should not be tolerated.

With this in mind, I have attempted to forward a number of criteria—uncertainty, irreversibility, catastrophic potential, and dependency—that would have allowed the hazards of pesticide production in Bhopal to have become more detectable. Most of the time these criteria are seen as possible outcomes that have to be accepted alongside any hazardous technology rather than used as bases for decision-making. This view must be changed. In order to insure that accidents like Bhopal do not repeat themselves, these criteria suggest the presentation of as many worst-case scenarios as possible associated with the use of chemical pesticides in order to make informed choices. They suggest that those most responsible for the rapid deployment of pesticides—the industries and governments involved in their production, import, and export—slow down the pace of this deployment and search for alternatives that are both safer and that do not return dependent populations to the conditions that existed before development. Above all, this debate must be public. We cannot tolerate the technocratic arrogance that suggests the public is too ignorant, apathetic, or inclined to overestimate risks to be included in decisions which fundamentally affect their well-being. We cannot allow a small group of self-interested elites decide what is best for the general population. Despite their undoubtedly good intentions, they do a disservice to themselves and to global political and economic relations when such a paternal attitude reigns.

Developing criteria that allow for basic detection of hazards before actual implementation of hazardous technologies is not a total solution to the problem. Detection itself, as we have seen, is no guarantee of safety, although it is the necessary first step. Without this basic capability—even if it means only a general and not specific knowledge of potential hazards—all further mitigation automatically fails. If, on the other hand, possibilities for detection are systematically widened, if full public participation becomes a reality, the choices that can be made to enhance the safety of pesticide technologies and prevent their hazards from being masked are also widened.

Notes

1. Fischhoff et al.'s (1981) work is a welcome exception to this and understands the importance of informing the public and involving it in the decision-making process (cf. especially pp. 137–140, 148–150).

2. Abnormal, that is, in the moral or pathological sense of that term, and not "non-normal" or "irregular" in the sense of statistical rarity or deviation from the mean.

3. Cf., for example, Douglas and Wildavsky's (1982) critique of irreversibility, pp. 21ff.

APPENDIX

The purpose of this appendix is to outline some of the general research orientations which informed the main body of the text. The study itself was guided by a firm belief in the value of methodological pluralism and pragmatism. Overly rigid adherence to a single method deemed by whatever criteria to be appropriate to the case at hand is never sufficient in itself to guarantee any more than a limited perspective on events of the type which unfolded in Bhopal. While I have drawn on principles of historical documentation and content analysis and their application to the case study, which I discuss here, I also have not hesitated to draw liberally from fields as diverse as critical theory and ordinary language analysis in order to shed further light on the problem (insofar as historical analysis is relevant to each of these fields). But I will spare the reader a lengthy philosophical discussion on the latter and note only that a truly interested and sympathetic depiction of the tragedy which is befalling the Third World in its drive for modernization must today acknowledge that any approach which promises to critically elucidate the hazards process in all its complexity is at least a *possible* candidate for enhancing our knowledge and should not be rejected outright. Certainly, the victims of Bhopal are not served by endless and dogmatic debates over the "one true" methodology for analysis.

In Chapters 2 and 3, I brought a number of theoretical reflections together that might account for limited possibilities for detecting hazards, the increasing hazardousness of the socio-physical environment, and the rising vulnerability of the world's poor to those hazards. Three general processes were isolated and offered as potential explanations—first, social defining processes for transforming perceptions of the safety of hazards and mitigations (cost-benefit decisions, setting thresholds, limiting causal chains, and non-decisions); second, processes of uncertainty and counter-finality present in mitigation; and third, global economic processes such as the separation of core and peripheral states that push for the transfer of hazardous technologies to Third World nations, determine the form of competition between and among states, create ideologies stressing economic and political stability, and influence the content of the regulation of hazardous technologies.

The general orienting framework I used in order to isolate and critically comment on these processes was the historical case study (cf. Stinchcombe 1978; Skocpol 1979). Specifically, I wanted to fashion a coherent historical context for the chain of events leading up to and culminating in the industrial disaster that took place in Bhopal, and to use this as a basis for further explicating what I considered to be the central concepts for an explanation.

The historical case study is primarily an exploratory methodology and its use is not intended as a direct test of hypotheses (cf. Skocpol 1979, p. 35; Stinchcombe 1978, p. 4). Rather, it occupies a strategic position in the process of theory building. As I have repeatedly argued, there are a diverse number of theoretical concepts which might be derived from various sociological orientations that are relevant to an explanation of the hazards process. The purpose of this study was not to develop a "test" of the applicability of such concepts, but to first use the combination of concepts as one possible framework for making sense of the tragedy. They enabled the description of the event in a particular way and from an *interested* point of view (cf. Habermas 1968, Chap. 1). Stinchcombe (1984, p. 4) employs an architectural metaphor to characterize this idea: "The value of the rooms (re: concepts) is that the historical facts fit in them, not that they have been derived from a general scheme for the building." The point is therefore to develop an interesting and theoretically informative account of the case under investigation. Realizing that the "facts" of the case may be arranged in an indefinite number of ways, the point of conducting an historical case study is to treat the case as the subject of a *possible* theory or set of reflections (Skocpol 1979. p. 35).

It has been legitimately argued that there are specific problems of generalizability, comparability, and interpretation when the case study method is employed (Saslow 1982, p. 12). I shall discuss each of these problems in the course of this appendix and merely state here that the case study, when properly used, can be a powerful tool for illustrating complex relationships in depth, for accounting for change over time, and for suggesting further areas of research.

Case studies are not all of one type, however—there are many alternatives involving subtle modifications of design. In my work on Bhopal, I employed a modified paradigm for the structuring of case research developed by

Riley (1963). To better defend some of the methodological choices I made, I will briefly comment on a few of these alternatives, which involve (1) the nature of the research case, (2) the number of cases, (3) the sociotemporal context of the study, (4) the choice of the case, (5) the time frame of the study, (6) the source of data, (7) the method of gathering data, and (8) methods of data analysis. From the alternatives possible within each category, I have chosen a design that I believe best illustrates the theoretical orientations developed in Chapters 2 and 3 and that accounts for certain practical constraints (of time and money) that I operated under. Limitations and advantages of the design choices I made will be discussed at each step.

The Nature of the Research Case

The general form of the case study is apparent in all forms of sociological research. Each research design must specify the type of case or cases that will broadly fit the outline of the theoretical model and the level of the social system that is the focus of the study (Riley 1963, p. 19). Cases may range from individuals in roles, to dyads, to groups or subgroups, to society or societies in general, to the global system as a whole (cf. Selltiz et al. 1959, Chap. 14; Merton 1957, Chapters 1-3). Cases may be taken from only one of these particular levels of the social system, from combinations of different levels, or from an analysis of case levels within the social system as a whole depending on the theoretical and practical needs of the investigator. Cases may include not only unique social objects (individuals, groups, etc.), but properties of these objects (roles, statuses, etc.) and relations among objects (e.g., power).

In short, the abstract notion of a case cuts across a number of different levels of sociological research and is applicable to a variety of different methodological strategies. Considerations concerning the nature of the research case or cases are just as relevant to survey research as to historical documentation. They are equally as relevant to experimental design as to participant observation. In each instance, the choice of empirical cases for study depends on the (pre-)conceptual model.

With regard to the disaster in Bhopal, a number of general reflections indicated that the relevant research case had to be the total system involved in the production and transfer of a hazardous technology—in this instance, chemical pesticides. Within this system, a set of abstract subsystems or case levels was distinguished—societies, groups and subgroups, and individuals in specific roles—whose theory-relevant relations varied with the categories of (1) the major independent variables (political defining processes, uncertainty and counterfinality, and global economic pressures), (2) the intervening variable (the possibility of detection, and (3) dependent variables (hazardousness and vulnerability).

In this study, case levels involved in the process of defining hazards and mitigations included individuals in specific roles (plant managers and operatives employed at Union Carbide of India's Bhopal facility, hazards exts. corporate board members and administrators of various regulatory agencies), and groups and subgroups (the corporate entity of Union Carbide and its subsidiary, Union Carbide of India, Ltd., along with the state government of Madhya Pradesh, where the city of Bhopal is located).

Problems of uncertainty in the Bhopal tragedy were manifest at all case levels from individuals (e.g., the lack of role-specific information for plant operatives), to groups (flows of information between parent and subsidiary corporations), to society as a whole (information regarding current and projected levels of agricultural production, the fluctuations in demand and price structure for pesticides, etc.). Counterfinality, on the other hand, involved the analysis of structural problems arising from the effects of individual actions on group processes, some examples of which were provided in Chapter 3.

Global economic factors were analyzed at the societal level within the overall system of producing and transferring pesticides. The relations between the United States and India with regard to agricultural development were of obvious importance here. In particular, I wished to examine societal level processes involved in the inter- and intranational regulations governing the use and export of pesticide technologies between core and peripheral states, and the function of these technologies in the desire of developing states for adequate food supplies and economic stability (cf. Wallerstein 1982; Skocpol 1979).

Detection possibilities are primarily the properties of individuals in roles. In the Bhopal accident, limited detection was seen not only in the behavior of those in the bastis surrounding Union Carbide's plant at the time of the accident, but also in the behavior of plant operatives, managers, scientists, state officials and corporate executives both prior and subsequent to the event.

Finally, hazardousness and vulnerability were analyzed at both the individual and group level, specifically with the intent of providing an explanation for the disproportionate losses incurred by the poor living in proximity to Union Carbide's plant at the time of the accident.

It is important to reemphasize that the research case for the present study is the *total* social system involved in the production and transfer of hazardous pesticide technologies from developed to developing states. Following Riley (1963, p. 19), the difficulties involved in a case study of this type do not stem from the complexity of the relations among different case levels. Many sociological studies involve analysis on a variety of case levels. Difficulties arise mainly in terms of maintaining consistent distinctions between levels and exercising care in making unwarranted inferences across levels (Simon 1969, p. 129). With the total system functioning as the research case, the advantages gained from the use of different levels lies in the ability to give a multiple perspective on a complex problem, i.e., to illustrate the problem in the broadest possible fashion from many different angles rather than attempt to prove a small number of conceptually narrow hypotheses. Perhaps even more importantly, this method gives a fuller accounting of what might be called the actual dynamics of social life, which is simultaneously composed of all the various levels we have been discussing.

The Number of Cases

Despite the heterogeneity of case levels, it can be said that this study focused on a single case—the system of pesticide production and transfer as it related to the chemical leak in Bhopal on 2 December 1984. I have not attempted to draw specific inferences to similar situations (i.e., industrial accidents) as they have occurred or might occur in other developing countries. Rather than providing a basis for inference that a comparative study might offer, I chose rather to concentrate on a description of a single event within the context of a global historical process.

It is usually argued that single descriptive case studies are severely limited in terms of their generalizability and that their fault lies in the fact that they are primarily exploratory. This does not imply, however, the complete absence of a model for analysis of the case, nor does it mean that the charge of "ad hocing," often laid upon descriptive case studies, is automatically valid. There is nothing to suggest that the analysis of a case from the standpoint of an admittedly preliminary set of theoretical reflections cannot generate "historically specific general ideas" from the case narrative or make specific recommendations regarding possibly similar cases (Stinchcombe 1978, p. 4). It does mean that social data are *actively* sought and elaborated on for the purpose of what Merton (1957, pp. 108–111) calls the recasting of theory. To state specifically the precise direction of hypothetical relations before the model is actually applied to the case would be to focus too early on aspects that may prove later to be superfluous. The intent of the present case study was to ask the reader to withhold judgment until the "broader view" was available. This broader view emerged only in the realization that the Bhopal accident was inevitably a part of a total system process, i.e., the system of pesticide production and transfer at a global level.

Focusing on the total system as the case had a number of additional advantages. First, it allowed the development of a wide range of detail. Rather than concentrating on a few select aspects of interest, the description of the total system allowed the gathering of a variety of data that would enable the reader to see actors in a complete life situation. The wealth of detail provides an immediacy to findings that are difficult to duplicate by any other research method.

Second, patterns of behavior that were not immediately obvious to participants became apparent in the description of the total system. Many of the workers at the Bhopal plant, for example, had little knowledge of the global factors that may have determined the perception of the hazards to which they and their community were exposed. Such latent aspects of social structure are not always visible in the findings generated by other more "standard" research methods, e.g., survey techniques.

Third, the total system as the case allowed me to grasp and assemble processes and patterns of action as a whole rather than in piecemeal fashion. The descriptive case study is sufficiently open-ended and instructive to prohibit excluding from attention any property that seems theoretically important as the research develops. Each phenomenon is examined within its total social context rather than being isolated and torn out of its setting (cf. Malinowski, 1926, p. 4).

The Sociotemporal Context of the Study

The primary options for choosing the sociotemporal context from which cases may be drawn are (1) a single social system within a given time frame, and (2) multiple social systems at different times. This study opted, with some misgivings, for the former.

Practical considerations of time and money were most important in making this choice. In the first case, I was a graduate student with very few resources when I embarked on this study. Secondly, data on industrial accidents are difficult to come by and were not systematized at the time of this writing. The expenses involved in collecting comparative data were generally prohibitive despite the obvious advantages of having access to such data. The Bhopal accident, in contrast, was fairly recent and received such intensive scrutiny in the media that data were relatively easy to obtain. The only other industrial accident in recent years that received so much attention was the Three Mile Island case, but the nature of that accident and the losses to populations were so different than Bhopal that a comparison of cases would have been quite difficult.

As I noted in the main body of the text, the number of industrial accidents with severe and relatively bounded consequences in this century is actually quite small. The Bhopal tragedy was the worst industrial accident ever to take place in terms of lives lost and numbers of people affected. In this sense it was a unique occurrence. Comparisons with other disasters of this type in which fewer persons were affected may thus be misleading.

The Bhopal tragedy was also significant in that it hooked up in rather explicit ways to the problem of industrial and agricultural development in the Third World, particularly to the vulnerability of the poor to technological choices that carry hazardous consequences. Industrial accidents do not limit themselves to poor countries, but the Bhopal incident drew the line between the differential class effects of hazards as perhaps no other technological disaster in this century could have. In this sense what happened in Bhopal did not as much *prove* a particular model of the hazards process as it *illustrated* this process in a particularly forceful manner.

The Choice of the Case

The concern of the present study was with the salience and importance of the Bhopal incident for filling out the conceptual model presented in Chapters 2 and 3, and for exploring how a particular chain of events and decisions fit or failed to fit this particular model. The purpose was to learn as much as possible about the properties of a particular hazards system in depth, i.e., through the interaction of a variety of case levels within the overall system.

Random sampling, despite its desirability for some forms of social research, was therefore not appropriate for this particular study. There are two reasons for this. First, the investigation of the Bhopal tragedy was undertaken here with a critical intent—critical of a process of technology transfer that had unintended but real consequences for the safety of the poor in developing nations. This does not imply that the descriptive content of this case study was biased. The goal was to remain as objective as possible in the description of the chain of events leading up to the Bhopal disaster. This description was then used to support (or reject) critical claims regarding the process as a whole.

Second, since major industrial accidents—in the sense of a high number of deaths or persons affected over the short term—are rather rare in the 20th century, a random sample of such events in this situation was not desirable from the point of view of a critical study such as this one, particularly if such a sample would by chance have excluded the most important of those events, i.e., Bhopal. The Bhopal case was not totally representative of industrial accidents in general, nor was it representative of other accidents in terms of overall losses (which are usually small). There is no way of telling a priori whether future accidents will repeat the exact pattern of Bhopal. In all likelihood they will not. This in no way, however, biases the conclusion that general ideas and recommendations can be developed from the Bhopal experience. In fact, the very magnitude and uniqueness of the Bhopal tragedy called out for such generalizations to possible future accidents involving the pesticide industry. From an ethical point of view, waiting for another tragedy similar to the Bhopal incident simply to gain the advantages of comparison seemed to me both timid and immoral. An in depth study of the hazards process at Bhopal (distinct from the actual mechanics of the disaster or the numbers of people killed or injured), combined with a conceptual model to help explain this process, helped to reveal in a critical way the roots of such accidents as they might occur in the future and possibly enable us to prevent them.

The Time Frame of the Study

The case researcher faces the alternatives of an investigation of a social system conducted at one point in time—a static or synchronic analysis—and one dealing with the dynamics of interaction and change over time—a diachronic analysis (Riley 1963, p. 21; cf. also Giddens 1979, Chap. 1). The present study placed the Bhopal tragedy within an historical context. The development of this context involved a mapping of changes in the network of hazards and vulnerabilities occasioned by India's agricultural and industrial development needs over the last 25 years up to the time of the actual accident (Farmer 1977, p. 1; Prasad 1983, pp. 82ff.; Chambers and Farmer 1977, pp. 413–421; Tewari 1982). Ramifications from the Bhopal tragedy continued to be felt as this essay was being written. The period subsequent to this writing will undoubtedly witness a number of issues—legal, political, medical—that will come into sharper focus as new developments arise from the accident. Because these issues are only now emerging and since they are to a large extent outside the scope of the present study, the analysis focused primarily on hazard processes that led up to and were involved in the actual accident itself. New developments will have to await further ongoing research.

The history of recent U.S. development aid to India ostensibly designed to bring the latter country into a self-sufficient and competitive position on the world market coincides with the global history of increasing hazardousness and vulnerability outlined in Chapter 3. For both processes the period from around 1960 to the present was critical. During that period, U.S. agricultural and industrial aid received its start in the form of increased funding and technical assistance from the U.S. AID Program (Super 1980, pp. 17–18). This was the time when new agricultural products were introduced to Indian farmers along with supporting land use, irrigation, fertilizer, and pesticide technologies. The purpose of these efforts was ostensibly to solve India's recurrent problems with food shortages. Solving the agricultural problem was supposed to provide the foundation for the industrial development India needed to eliminate widespread poverty and to bring the country to a competitive level on par with other Western nations (Bowonder et al. 1985, p. 7).

As we have seen, this overall program of agricultural development came to be known as the Green Revolution. Over the last 20 years, since around 1966, the Green Revolution has seen its ups and downs, not only in terms of its effects on actual foodstuff production (which has been variable but generally positive), but also in terms of its effects on changing the Indian society. In the latter case the results have been depressing, and massive poverty remains despite the industrialization that has followed agricultural reforms (Farmer 1977, pp. 1–2). Critics have charged that the Green Revolution failed to the extent that social and cultural changes were not given the necessary attention that changes in the economic structure of agriculture and industry required (Ember 1985).

Along with U.S. government involvement came increased corporate involvement. I traced this involvement with regard to the history of Union Carbide's role in the manufacture of pesticides to support the increased production made possible by the introduction of new varieties of seed grains. How this process evolved with regard to changing definitions of hazards and mitigations, uncertainty and counterfinality, and global pressures for modernization, was the primary focus of the historical analysis. Specifically, the question was posed of how this process changed the overall level of hazardousness and vulnerability of the community of Bhopal, and how the possibilities of detection of the hazards involved in pesticide production were altered and limited over time.

The advantage of an historical study lies in this ability to document change over time. This is particularly important in a study designed to map changes in the network of hazards and mitigations associated with a given productive technology. Negotiations between the U.S. and Indian governments, Union Carbide and its subsidiary (Union Carbide of India, Ltd.), among plant operatives, and within the community of Bhopal itself were in a constant state of flux regarding appropriate methods of development from the early 1960's onward. The perception of pesticide production alternated continually between its hazardous and mitigative possibilities during this time and was dependent on technical and practical decisions, uncertainties, and global pressures. For the most part, the poor in Bhopal were excluded from these negotiations and could do little to alter the changes in hazards in their environment that were occurring all around them (Ramaseshan 1985b, pp. 37–40; Bidwai 1985d, p. 28)

Data Sources

Sociological data are traditionally divided into primary and secondary sources (Kendall and Lazarsfeld 1950). Primary data includes information derived from structured interviews, participant observation, experiments, and the like. Secondary data, on the other hand, includes information taken from personal or historical documents, census reports, newspaper accounts, or scholarly reports generated by individuals other than the investigator.

A principal advantage of utilizing primary data lies in the fact that it is collected specifically for the purpose of the investigation. It is argued that the researcher is thus able to exercise some control over how the data is to be gathered and interpreted (Simon 1969, Chapter 21). Secondary data, on the other hand, is often criticized for failing to meet these standards. The investigator who employs secondary sources of data, particularly in the form of historical documents, is often criticized for being unable to account for specific biases that may arise in the collection of the data, or the theoretical or practical purposes that may have motivated their original use.

Until recently, this was the accepted sociological wisdom—primary sources of data clearly are better than secondary sources in terms of their reliability and validity for making inferences. Methodological reflections over the past years have indicated, however, that this may not entirely be the case (cf. Platt 1981, pp. 65–67). Skocpol (1978) has argued convincingly that important sociological conclusions can be reached through careful analysis of historical documents. Further, both primary and secondary data clearly involve hermeneutical problems (Stinchcombe 1978, p. 5). Regardless of the question of how data are gathered, all sociologists are confronted with the symbolic nature of reports about human activities, attitudes, motives, etc. From this perspective, it makes little difference whether these reports are generated by survey techniques, experimental manipulations, or whether they are in the form of historical documents—each requires interpretive competencies of the investigator no matter how many hands the data have passed through. In any case, primary data derived from surveys, for example, face the same difficulty in that the principle investigator is rarely the individual who collects and systematizes the original data.

Secondary sources of data may in fact have distinct advantages over the use of primary sources. Biases that result from the mere presence of the investigator in the relevant social setting are not longer a factor although, admittedly, the problem reproduces itself at another level when dealing with second hand reports. Not all "secondary" documents contain this form of bias, however. Much of the present case study utilized verbatim reports of Union Carbide executives, plant operatives, and state officials. This bypassed to some extent the problem of selectivity inevitably introduced by newspaper editors and reports interested in obtaining only the most dramatic aspects of the event (cf. Gitlin 1980, pp. 249–252; Gans 1979, pp. 78 ff.). I shall report to this point below.

Some of the data used in the case study were generated from a systematic library search of scholarly reports directly and indirectly related to the Bhopal incident or the process of transfer of hazardous materials and technologies to the Third World. In this case, methods of data gathering involved research processes similar to how investigators operate in actual field situations (cf. Glassner and Corzine 1980, pp. 305–306). Much of the initial work focused on the development of library "sites" containing topic areas relevant to the theoretical issues raised in Chapters 2 and 3. Relevant sites for this study included past studies on pesticide and chemical regulations, articles on the place of the Green Revolution in India's agriculture, political negotiations involved in hazardous technology transfers, and the place of the poor in India's economy. Within each site, a selection of articles and reports was chosen based on their theoretical relevance to the Bhopal incident. The problem of selection itself was greatly reduced by the fact that the tragedy in Bhopal was a fairly recent occurrence, and scholarly reports and analyses are still quite limited, although several book length treatments have since appeared and were incorporated into the analysis.

The majority of data were generated from a systematic examination of the newspaper reports that followed the disaster. Due to the recency of the disaster, newspaper reports contain most of the basic information and analyses we currently have to document the events at Bhopal. Following the Bhopal accident, there was substantial coverage of events in the world press of varying depth and quality. Newspaper accounts are naturally biased by constraints of journalistic interest, the nature of the events with which they deal, and social conditions external to the organization of journalistic accounts (Gans 1979, pp. 78–80). Gitlin (1980, pp. 258–269) has further argued that the production of news can operate to reinforce existing patterns of hegemony in society by profoundly altering the framework in which events are perceived by the public. The importance of these considerations cannot be underestimated. Nonetheless, several accounts of the Bhopal accident have been noteworthy for the care they have taken to present an overall perspective on the tragedy along with a comprehensive analysis, and this was a general criterion for selecting among the many newspaper articles dealing with the event. The series of articles appearing in the *New York Times* in January and February of 1985 was chosen on this basis.

To guard against cultural bias that might develop from the exclusive use of an American newspaper, articles and analyses were also examined from a variety of other sources, notably those appearing in the Indian press. A compilation of many of these articles has recently appeared and is available from Arena Press (1985). Such articles were particularly invaluable for gaining insights into different defining procedures involved in the hazards process. For instance, what counted as a mitigation from the cultural perspective of the exporting country (as indicated by press reports) sometimes counted as a hazard from the point of view of the importing country, and vice-versa. Utilizing a comparative cultural base of journalistic accounts as I attempted to do here had the dual advantage of making one both aware of journalistic reporting biases as well as providing a depth of coverage from a variety of views that would be unavailable if only one newspaper source were examined.

Finally, it is worth noting again that scholarly summaries of the Bhopal accident are quite rare at the time of this writing. This is understandable given the recency of the event. I relied a great deal on Bowonder et al.'s analysis of the tragedy published in *Environment* in September of 1985. An article by Robert Engler appearing in *The Nation* (27 April 1985) has also been valuable, particularly for its critical insights into both Bhopal and the global production of chemicals in general. On occasion, I have additionally relied on conversations with scholars who have works in progress on aspects of the tragedy which will undoubtedly become available in the future as the debate surrounding Bhopal grows.

Data Analysis

Content analysis furnished the specific method I employed to systematize, summarize and interpret the wide range of reports collected for the case study. Stone et al. (1966, p. 5) have defined content analysis as "any research technique for making inferences by systematically and objectively identifying specific characteristics within texts." Specifically, I examined individual texts for references to social defining processes (cost/benefit decisions, limiting causal chains, establishing thresholds, and circumscribing the ability to detect hazards), uncertainties and counterfinality, and global economic pressures (regulations involving the transfer of pesticides, competition among states, desires for economic stability, etc.). Additionally, I examined texts for references that allowed me to infer how these processes are linked to increasing hazardousness and vulnerability of the poor.

Successful inference in content analysis depends on developing adequate categories to locate and classify diverse textual references. One method of dealing with this problem involves a search for key words or phrases in the text that reflect relevant aspects of the theoretical variables. For instance, in searching for texts that illustrated the idea of limiting causal chains, I attempted to pick out phrases that suggested the idea that "adequate precautions" had been taken to insure against an accident—e.g., "Everything possible was done to insure safety mechanism x functioned properly," or "Only a limited amount of redundancy can be incorporated into the system to insure safety." Similarly, for uncertainty, I developed a category that selected phrases referring to a "lack of information"—e.g., "The plant operator could not have known of the malfunction, because warning device x was inoperative at the time," etc.

Categories developed for the investigation had to be appropriate to the theoretical variables of interest in Chapters 2 and 3. In order to do this, I took a sample of the various articles, books, etc., I had collected and conducted a search for relevant textual words or phrases. The search itself involved the use of a thesaurus to set up semantic equivalences between theoretical concepts, general categories, and the actual texts that were used.

I proceeded by first reading each text in the sample in its entirety for its overall thrust. This was followed by a second reading in which the text was divided into various "sectors" (sentences, paragraphs, phrases, quotes, etc.) that seemed to indicate a unitary concept or idea. These formed, with the aid of the thesaurus to establish semantic equivalences, the basic categories for the analysis of the remainder of the texts. These categories are summarized in Figure A.1.

The next step in the procedure was to gather the categories (which had been written in the margins of each text) and group them into sets that I thought were relevant to my tentative theoretical concepts. This was the most difficult part of the procedure and required a degree of interpretation for which the thesaurus was only of limited help. Rather than working "up" from the categories to the theoretical concepts that they might indicate, I had to work "down" from these concepts and interpret the categories I had developed from my reading as instances subsumed under these concepts. The thesaurus was not useful, for instance, in making the link between "adequate precautions" and the concept of limiting causal chains. This link had to be made rather through the sensible context of the theoretical discussion itself. In that discussion, limiting causal chains referred to the idea of cutting off hazardous sequences of a production process at a point where little else could be done to insure safety. This suggested the notion that existing safety precautions were in a sense "adequate" or at least bounded or closed off by the system as it was defined ("system closure" and "system boundaries" are additional categories of the concept of limiting causal chains in Fig. A.1).

FIGURE A.1. Semantic categories for content analysis

COST-BENEFIT DECISIONS
  profitability considerations
  economic tradeoffs

LIMITING CAUSAL CHAINS
  adequate precautions
  system closure
  system boundaries

SETTING THRESHOLDS
  hazard potentials
  levels of risk/safety

NON-DECISIONS
  limiting agendas
  issue blockage

UNCERTAINTY
  lack of information
  information handling
    difficulties
  information processing
    difficulties

COUNTERFINALITY
  negative outcomes
  increased hazard
    potential

DETECTION POSSIBILITIES
  hazard perception
  hazard recognition
  hazard determination
  hazard assessment

GLOBAL ECONOMIC FACTORS
  industry regulation
  pressures for the
    adoption of
    technologies
  national concerns for
    self-sufficiency
  state--industry regulations

HAZARDOUSNESS
  personal harm
  potential loss
  degree of risk

VULNERABILITY
  inadequate resources
  inability to respond
  safety limitations

In short, the content analysis used in this study involved a continual and open-ended shift from text to category to concept. The whole process involved several rereadings of the texts depending on, among other things, the ease or difficulty they presented for interpretation in view of the preliminary theory. The end result of this process was the reconstructed history of the Bhopal tragedy that was given in Chapter 1.

Not all portions of the text were categorized. These portions were simply not applicable to my theoretical concerns and I made no attempt to force a fit between these and the concepts I developed in Chapters 2 and 3.

Several articles, for example, referred to legal issues that developed subsequent to the accident. These issues are obviously important to any discussion of the Bhopal incident, but were not considered relevant to my interests.

Content analysis may be either quantitative or qualitative (Stone et al. 1966, p. 6). In the former instance, the usual procedure involves counting the number of occurrences of a given text in relation to each category and applying statistical calculations such as chi-square to the resulting summations. The approach taken in the present study, however, was qualitative. My interest, as noted above, was not so much in the direct test of hypotheses but was rather more exploratory and illustrative in nature. I was not concerned so much with the frequency of occurrence of given texts but with the use of these texts to identify and understand in as broad a manner as possible the operation of the hazard process (cf. Stinchcombe 1978, p. 5). The texts themselves, regardless of their frequency, demonstrated the processes of political negotiation and defining that alter the perception of hazards.

The elements in the text often suggested possible omissions or necessary revisions in the initial model. But for the purposes of this work the number of occurrences of a given text could not be automatically assumed to be a reliable guide to its theoretical importance. This is all the more true of newspaper accounts which often tended to overemphasize the spectacular and immediate consequences of the Bhopal tragedy at the expense of covering historical, global, or structural causes. It is the latter that I was theoretically most interested in. Therefore, textual items that dealt with these latter factors were accorded more systematic weight regardless of the number of times they appeared in accounts.

Throughout the process I intended to be especially aware of those textual passages that systematically linked definitional, structural, and global hazards processes to the problems of detectability, hazardousness and vulnerability. Some of these passages were counterfactual in nature—e.g., "If the poor would have known the extent of the hazards involved in pesticide production, many lives could have been saved," or "If the state government would not have allowed Union Carbide to locate in a heavily populated area, the disaster might have been averted." Statements such as these, based upon a retrospective analysis of the hazard, formed important links among theoretical variables in this study. At the same time they offered important evidence of an ongoing process of definition that could set the boundaries for future hazards.

Conclusions

The primary point of this appendix was to stress that the present study did not attempt a rigorous test of hypotheses in the classical sense. In general, the field of hazards research has as yet no developed general theory to explain the phenomena of increasing hazardousness of the sociophysical environment or differential vulnerabilities to hazards. In this sense, the theory of these phenomena sketched in Chapters 2 and 3 is unique, but it is also tentative. More importantly, the goal of this study was to utilize a range of sociological concepts derived from a variety of perspectives— social defining processes, uncertainty and counterfinality and global economy—to illuminate the processes involved in the Bhopal tragedy rather than use the Bhopal accident merely to test various propositions derived from these perspectives. Of course, focusing on one case of the hazards process occurring at one time is not an adequate test of theory. This was never my goal. Rather, it is maintained that only by focusing on as many system elements as possible can one adequately understand what took place in Bhopal and use this information as an explicit guide for making recommendations that might insure that such a tragedy will not repeat itself. The point, if I may paraphrase Marx, is to not only theorize about the world but to change it.

Therefore I have undertaken to examine the Bhopal tragedy through the use of a very open-ended framework, concentrating on a broad range of micro- and macrosocial processes. This implied taking into account the total system of relations impinging on the Bhopal incident and organizing the events of Bhopal in terms of their relevance to this total system. Whether the overall theoretical system employed here is correct or not, the value of using such a system comes in its ability to suggest new and novel ways of viewing accidents such as the one occurred in Bhopal.

It would have been desirable to have been able to conduct a comparative study, i.e., one in which the features of the Bhopal accident were contrasted with other technological disasters, but time and resource considerations prohibited this. Also, since the Bhopal tragedy was the worst industrial catastrophe in history in terms of lives lost and person affected, it was in a real sense unique, and comparison to other industrial accidents would be tenuous at best. Most important, however, is the current relevance of the Bhopal tragedy. Analyses of the event are only now beginning to come in, and Bhopal promises to produce more systematic information than any other prior accident involving the chemical industry. The topic is (unfortunately) relevant. It is tragic that this relevance came at the expense of so many lives.

BIBLIOGRAPHY

Amin, Samir. 1982. "Crisis, Nationalism and Socialism." Pp. 167–231 in *Dynamics of Global Crisis*. New York: Monthly Review Press.

Anderson, William A. 1969. "Disaster Warning and Communication Processes in Two Communities." *The Journal of Communication* 19 (June): 92–104.

Arrow, K. and L. Hurwicz. 1972. "An Optimality Criterion for Decision-Making Under Uncertainty." In C. F. Carter and J. L. Ford (eds.), *Uncertainty and Expectation in Economics*. Clifton, N.J.: Kelley.

Bachrach, Peter and Morton Baratz. 1963. "Decisions and Non-Decisions: An Analytical Framework." *American Political Science Review* 57 (September): 632–642.

———. 1970. *Power and Poverty*. New York: Oxford.

Bandyopadhyay, Jayanta. 1985. "Technological Terrorism." Pp. 91–94 in *Bhopal: Industrial Genocide?* Hong Kong: Arena Press.

Banerjee, Brohendra Nath. 1986 *Bhopal Gas Tragedy—Accident or Experiment?* Paribus Publishers and Distributors (New Dehli).

Baran, Paul A. 1957. *The Political Economy of Growth*. New York: Monthly Review Press.

Barkun, Michael. 1977. "Disaster in History." *Mass Emergencies* 2: 219–231.

Barton, Allen H. 1970. *Communities in Disaster*. New York: Anchor Books.

Benveniste, Guy. 1977. *The Politics of Expertise*. San Francisco: Boyd and Fraser.

Bhandari, Arvind. 1985a. "Aspects of the Bhopal Tragedy." Pp. 102–106 in *Bhopal: Industrial Genocide?* Hong Kong: Arena Press.

———. 1985b. "The Avaricious Giants." Pp. 114–118 in *Bhopal: Industrial Genocide?* Hong Kong: Arena Press.

Bidwai, Prafal. 1985a. "What Caused the Pressure Build-Up?" Pp. 57–62 in *Bhopal: Industrial Genocide?* Hong Kong: Arena Press.

———. 1985b. "Plant Design Badly Flawed." Pp. 63–69 in *Bhopal: Industrial Genocide?* Hong Kong: Arena Press.

———. 1985c. "Plant Undermanned, Run Down." Pp. 70–74 in *Bhopal: Industrial Genocide?* Hong Kong: Arena Press.

———. 1985d. "The Poisoned City—Diary from Bhopal." Pp. 26–34 in *Bhopal: Industrial Genocide?* Hong Kong: Arena Press.

Bluestone, Barry and Bennett Harrison. 1982. *The Deindustrialization of America*. New York: Basic Books.

Bogard, William. 1986. "Unacknowledged Conditions and Unanticipated Consequences of Hazards Mitigation." Paper presented at 1986 Western Social Science Meetings, Reno, Nevada (April).

Bowonder, B., Jeanne X. Kasperson and Roger E. Kasperson. 1985. "Avoiding Future Bhopals." *Environment* 27(7), September.

Breznitz, Shlomo. 1984. *Cry Wolf: The Psychology of False Alarms.* Hillsdale, N.J.: Lawrence Erlbaum, Assoc.

Burton, Ian, Robert W. Kates, and Gilbert F. White. 1978. *The Environment as Hazard.* New York: Oxford University Press.

Carson, Rachel. 1962. *Silent Spring.* Greenwich, Connecticut: Fawcett.

Chambers, Robert and B. H. Farmer. 1977. "Perceptions, Technology, and the Future." Pp. 413–421 in *Green Revolution?* edited by G. H. Farmer. Boulder, Colorado: Westview Press.

Chambers, Robert, H. D. Dias, Barbara Harris and John Harris. 1977b. "The Crisis and the Future." Pp. 377–397 in *Green Revolution?* edited by B. H. Farmer. Boulder, Colorado: Westview Press.

Dacy, Douglas C. and Howard Kunreuther. 1969. *The Economics of Natural Disasters.* New York: The Free Press.

Davenport, S. 1978. "Human Response to Hurricanes in Texas: Two Studies." Working paper no. 34. Boulder: Institute of Behavioral Science, University of Colorado.

De Grazia, Alfred. 1985. A *Cloud Over Bhopal: Causes, Consequences, and Constructive Solutions.* Bombay: Popular Prakashan Private Limited.

Dehli Science Forum. 1985. "Bhopal Tragedy: Looking Beyond." Report of the Dehli Science Forum Team to the international press in *Bhopal: Industrial Genocide?* Hong Kong: Arena Press.

De Saussure, Ferdinand. 1986. *Course in General Linguistics.* La Salle, Illinois: Open Court.

Diamond, P. and M. Rotschild (eds.). 1978. *Uncertainty in Economics.* New York: Academic Press.

Diamond, Stuart. 1985a. "The Bhopal Disaster: How It Happened." *New York Times,* 28 January.

———. 1985b. "The Disaster in Bhopal: Workers Recall Horror." *New York Times,* 30 January.

———. 1985c. "The Disaster in Bhopal: Lessons for the Future." *New York Times,* 3 February.

Diggory, James C. 1956. "Some Consequences of Proximity to a Disaster Threat." *Sociometry* 19 (March): 47–53.

Douglas, Mary and Aaron Wildavsky. 1982. *Risk and Culture.* Berkeley: University of California Press.

D'Souza, Frances. 1980. *Nuclear Reactors: Factors Associated with Stress in the Local Community,* London: International Disaster Institute.

Dynes, Russell R. 1970. *Organized Behavior in Disaster.* Lexington, Massachusetts: D. C. Heath and Col.

Edelman, Murray. 1964. *The Symbolic Uses of Politics.* Urbana: University of Illinois Press.

———. 1971. *Politics as Symbolic Action.* New York: Academic Press.

Ellul, Jacques. 1964. *The Technological Society.* New York: Vintage.

Elster, Jon. 1978. *Logic and Society: Contradictions and Possible Worlds.* Chichester: John Wiley and Sons.

———. 1983. *Explaining Technical Change.* Cambridge: Cambridge University Press.

Ember, Lois R. 1985. "Technology in India: an Uneasy Balance of Progress and Tradition." *Chemical and Engineering News* 11 (February).

Engler, Robert. 1985. "Many Bhopals: Technology Out of Control." *The Nation,* 27 April: 488–500.

Erikson, Kai T. 1976. *Everything in its Path.* New York: Simon and Schuster.

Everest, Larry. 1985. *Behind the Poison Cloud: Union Carbide's Bhopal Massacre.* Chicago: Banner Press.

Farmer, G. H. 1977. "Technology and Change in Rice-Growing Areas." Pp. 1–6 in *Green Revolution?* edited by B. H. Farmer. Boulder, Colorado: Westview Press.

Fera, Ivan. 1985. "The Day After." Pp. 48–55 in *Bhopal: Industrial Genocide?* Hong Kong: Arena Press.

Fischhoff, Baruch, Sara Lichtenstein, Paul Slovic, Stephen L. Derby, and Ralph L. Keeney. 1981. *Acceptable Risk.* Cambridge: Cambridge University Press.

Food and Agriculture Organization. 1979. *Trade Year Book.* Vol. 33. Rome: FAO-UN.

Friedman, D. G. 1975. *Computer Simulation in Natural Hazard Assessment.* Boulder, Colorado: Institute of Behavioral Science, University of Colorado.

Friedsam, H. J. 1962. "Older Persons in Disaster." Pp. 151–184 in *Man and Society in Disaster,* edited by George W. Baker and Dwight W. Chapman. New York: Basic Books.

Gabor, T. and T. K. Griffith. 1980. "The Assessment of Community Vulnerability to Acute Hazardous Materials Incidents." *Journal of Hazardous Materials* 3: 323–333.

Gans, Herbert. 1979. *Deciding What's News.* New York: Pantheon.

Gaya, Javed. 1985. "Corporate Criminal Liability, the New Dimension." Pp. 168–173 in *Bhopal: Industrial Genocide?* Hong Kong: Arena Press.

Giddens, Anthony. 1979. *Central Problems in Social Theory: Action, Structure and Contradiction in Social Analysis.* Berkeley: University of California Press.

Gitlin, Todd. 1980. *The Whole World Is Watching.* Berkeley: University of California Press.

Glassner, Barry and Jay Corzine. 1980. "Library Research as Fieldwork: a Strategy for Qualitative Content Analysis." *Sociology and Social Research* 66(3): 305–319.

Goffman, Erving. 1959. *The Presentation of Self in Everyday Life*. Garden City, N.Y.: Doubleday.

Goodwin, R. 1978. "Uncertainty as an Excuse for Cheating Our Children: The Case of Nuclear Waste." *Policy Sciences* 10: 25–43.

Goyal, K. N. 1985. "Bhopal Holocaust and the Law." Pp. 163–167 in *Bhopal: Industrial Genocide?* Hong Kong: Arena Press.

Graham, W. J. and C. A. Brown. 1983. "The Lawn Lake Dam Failure: a Description of the Major Flooding Events and an Evaluation of the Warning Process." Denver: Bureau of Reclamation.

Gray, Jane. 1981. "Characteristic Patterns of and Variations in Community Response to Acute Chemical Emergencies." *Journal of Hazardous Materials* 4: 357–365.

Greene, M., R. Perry and M. Lindell. 1981. "The March 1980 Eruptions of Mt. St. Helens: Citizen Perceptions of Volcano Threat." *Disaster* 5(1): 49–66.

Gruntfest, Eve, Thomas E. Downing and Gilbert F. White. 1978. "Big Thompson Flood Exposes Need for Better Flood Reaction System to Save Lives." *Civil Engineering* ASCE 48: 72–77.

Gupta, Y. P. 1985. "Poison Around and Within Us: Hazards of Growing Pesticide Use." Pp. 150–154 in *Bhopal: Industrial Genocide?* Hong Kong: Arena Press.

Habermas, Jurgen. 1984. *The Theory of Communicative Action, Vol. 1: Reason and the Rationalization of Society*. Boston: Beacon Press.

————. 1968. *Knowledge and Human Interests*. Boston: Beacon Press.

Hagman, Gunnar. 1984. *Prevention Better than Cure*. Stockholm: Swedish Red Cross.

Henry, Claude. 1974. "Investment Decisions Under Uncertainty: The Irreversibility Effect." *American Economic Review* 64: 1006–1012.

Hewitt, K. (editor). 1983. *Interpretations of Calamity*. Boston: Allen and Unwin.

Hewitt, Kenneth and Ian Burton. 1971. *The Hazardousness of a Place*. Department of Geography Research Publication No. 6. Toronto: University of Toronto.

Hopkins, Terence. 1979. *Processes of the World System*. Beverly Hills, CA: Sage.

Hutton, Janice R. 1976. "The Differential Distribution of Death in Disaster: a Test of Theoretical Propositions." *Mass Emergencies* 1 (October): 261–266.

Jeffery, Susan E. 1982. "The Creation of Vulnerability to Natural Disaster: Case Studies from the Dominican Republic." *Disasters* 6(1): 38–43.

Kasperson, Roger E. 1977. "Societal Managment of Technological Hazards." Pp. 49–80 in *Managing Technological Hazards: Research Needs and Opportunities*. Edited by Robert W. Kates. University of Colorado: Institute of Behavioral Science.

Kates, Robert W. (ed.). 1977. *Managing Technological Hazards: Research Needs and Opportunities*. University of Colorado: Institute of Behavioral Science.

Kendall, Patricia L. and Paul F. Lazarsfeld. 1950. "Problems of Survey Analysis." Pp. 133–196 in *Continuities in Social Research*, edited by R. K. Merton and P. F. Lazarzfeld. New York: Free Press.

Kottary, Sailish. 1985. "Whose Life is it Anyway?" *The Illustrated Weekly of India*, 30 December–5 January.

Kumar, C. Dera and S. K. Mukerjee. 1985. "Methyl Isocyanate: Profile of a Killer Gas." Pp. 125–134 in *Bhopal: Industrial Genocide?* Hong Kong: Arena Press.

Kurzman, Dan. 1987. A *Killing Wind: Inside Union Carbide and the Bhopal Disaster*. New York: McGraw-Hill.

Lagadec, Patrick. 1982. *Major Technological Risk: an Assessment of Industrial Disasters*. New York: Pergammon Press.

Leaning, Jennifer and Langley Keyes (eds.). 1984. *The Counterfeit Ark: Crisis Relocation for Nuclear War*. Cambridge, Mass.: Ballinger Publishing Co.

Lewis, J. 1979. "The Vulnerable State: an Alternative View." In *Disaster Assistance: Appraisal, Reform and New Approaches*. Edited by L. H. Stevens and S. J. Green. New York: New York University Press.

Lowrance, W. W. 1976. *Of Acceptable Risk: Science and the Determination of Safety*. Los Altos, California: William Kaufmann.

Lovins, Amory. 1979. *The Energy Controversy: Soft Path Questions and Answers*. San Francisco: Friends of the Earth.

Luce, R. D. and H. Raiffa. 1957. *Games and Decisions*. New York: Wiley.

Lueck, Thomas J. 1985. "Carbide Says Its Investigation Has Found Irregularities." *New York Times*, 28 January.

Lukes, Steven. 1974. *Power: A Radical View*. London: MacMillan.

Mack, Raymond W. and George W. Baker. 1961. *The Occasion Instant*. National Academy of Sciences, National Research Council Disaster Study 15. Washington, D.C.

Malinowski, Bronislaw. 1926. *Crime and Custom in Savage Society*. New York: Harcourt, Brace and World.

Marx, Karl. 1967. *Capital*, Vol. 3. New York: International Publishers.

Menon, Sadanand. 1985. "Second Mild Exposure to MIC Could Be Lethal Says Doctor." Pp. 135–137 in *Bhopal: Industrial Genocide?* Hong Kong: Arena Press.

Merton, Robert K. 1957. *Social Theory and Social Structure*. Glencoe, Illinois: The Free Press.

Mileti, Dennis S. 1980. "Human Adjustment to the Risk of Environmental Extremes." *Sociology and Social Research* 64(3): 327–347.

Mileti, Dennis S. and E. M. Beck. 1975. "Communication in Crisis: Explaining Evacuation Symbolically." *Communication Research* 2(January): 24–49.

Mileti, Dennis S., T. Drabek and J. Haas. 1975. *Human Systems in Extreme Environments: a Sociological Perspective.* Boulder, Colorado: University of Colorado Institute of Behavioral Sciences, Monograph 2.

Mileti, Dennis S., Janice R. Hutton and John S. Sorenson. 1981. *Earthquake Prediction Response and Options for Public Policy.* Boulder, Colorado: Institute of Behavioral Science, University of Colorado.

Mileti, Dennis, John Sorenson, and William Bogard. 1985. "Evacuation Decision-Making: Process and Uncertainty." Prepared by Oak Ridge National Laboratory for U.S. Department of Energy. Contract no. DE-AC05-840R21400.

Milliman, Jerome W. 1982. "Economic Issues in Formulating Policy for Earthquake Hazard Mitigations." Prepared for NSF workshop on hazards research, policy development and implementation incentives. University of Redlands: Redlands California.

Mojumder, M. N. 1985. "Away With All Pest." Pp. 145–149 in *Bhopal: Industrial Genocide?* Hong Kong: Arena Press.

Moore, Harry Estill. 1964. *. . . And the Winds Blew.* Austin, Texas: The Hogg Foundation for Mental Health, University of Texas.

New York Times, 1985a. "U.S. Company Said to Have Had Control in Bhopal." 28 January.

————. 1985b. "Company's Statement: the Major Points." 28 January.

————. 1985c. "Most at Plant Thought Poison Was Chiefly Skin-Eye Irritant." 30 January.

————. 1985d. "Slum Dwellers Unaware of Danger." 31 January.

————. 1985e. "Pesticide Plant Started as Showpiece but Ran Into Trouble." 3 February.

Norris, Ruth (editor). 1982. *Pills, Pesticides and Profits: The International Trade in Toxic Substances.* Croton-on-Hudson, New York: North River Press, Inc.

O'Connor, James. 1973. *The Fiscal Crisis of the State.* New York: St. Martin's Press.

Olson, Richard Stuart and Douglas C. Nilson. 1982. "Public Policy Analysis and Hazards Research: Natural Compliments." *The Social Science Journal* 19(1) January: 89–103.

Palm, Risa. 1985. "Geography and Consumer Protection: Housing Market Response to Earthquake Hazards Disclosure." *Southeastern Geographer* 25(1): 63–73.

Pankhurst, Anula. 1984. "Vulnerable Groups." *Disasters*, 3 August: 206–213.

Pelanda, Carlo. 1982. "Disaster and Sociosystemic Vulnerability." Pp. 67–91 in *The Social and Economic Aspects of Earthquakes: Proceedings of the 3rd International Conference.* Edited by Barclay G. Jones and Miha Tomazevic. Bled, Yugoslavia.

Perrow, Charles. 1984. *Normal Accidents: Living With High Risk Technologies.* New York: Basic Books.

Perry, Ronald W., and Marjorie R. Greene and Michael K. Lindell. 1980. "Enhancing Evacuation Warning Compliance: Suggestions for Emergency Planning." *Disasters* 4(4): 433–449.

Perry, Ronald W. and Alvin Mushkatel. 1984. *Disaster Management: Warning Response and Community Relocation.* Westport, Connecticutt: Quorum Books.

Perry, Ronald W., Michael K. Lindell and Marjorie R. Greene. 1981. *Evacuation and Emergency Management.* Lexington, Massachusetts and Toronto: Lexington Books.

Perry, Ronald W., Michael K. Lindell and Marjorie R. Greene. 1982. "Crisis Communications: Ethnic Differentials in Interpreting and Acting on Disaster Warnings." *Social Behavior and Personality* 10(1): 97–104.

Platt, Jennifer. 1981. "Evidence and Proof in Documentary Research: Some Specific Problems of Documentary Research." *Sociological Review* 29(1): 31–67.

Prasad, K. N. 1983. *Problems of Indian Economic Development: National and Regional Dimensions.* New Dehli: Sterling Publishers.

Press Trust of India. 1985. "Carbide's War Gas Tests Right Under DST's Nose!" Pp. 140–142 in *Bhopal: Industrial Genocide?* Hong Kong: Arena Press.

Quarantelli, E. L. 1974. *Disasters: Theory and Research.* Beverly Hills, California: Sage Publications.

Ramaseshan, Radhika. 1985a. "Government Responsibility for Bhopal Gas Tragedy." Pp. 95–101 in *Bhopal: Industrial Genocide?* Hong Kong: Arena Press.

———. 1985b. "Profit Against Safety." Pp. 35–47 in *Bhopal: Industrial Genocide?* Hong Kong: Arena Press.

Reinhold. Robert. 1985. "Disaster in Bhopal: Where Does Blame Lie?" *New York Times*, 31 January.

Rele, Subash J. 1985. "Dumping Ground for Pesticides." Pp. 155–159 in *Bhopal, Industrial Genocide?* Hong Kong: Arena Press.

Report of the Dehli Science Forum Team. 1985. "Bhopal Tragedy: Looking Beyond." Pp. 190–215 in *Bhopal: Industrial Genocide?* Hong Kong: Arena Press.

Riley, Matilda White. 1963. *Sociological Research: a Case Approach.* New York: Harcourt, Brace and World, Inc.

Rossi, Peter H., James D. Wright and Eleanor Weber-Burdin. 1982. *Natural Hazards and Public Choice: The State and Local Politics of Hazard Mitigation.* New York: Academic Press.

Rout, M. K. 1985. "The Bhopal Tragedy: Analysis of Related Issues." Bhutaneswar: Orissa State Prevention and Control of Pollution Board.

Saarinen, Thomas F. (ed.). 1982. *Perspectives on Increasing Hazard Awareness.* Boulder, Colorado: Institute of Behavioral Science, The University of Colorado.

Saarinen, Thomas F., Victor R. Baker, Robert Durrenberger and Thomas Maddock. 1984. "The Tucson, Arizona Flood of October 1983." National Research Council, Washington, D.C.: National Academy Press.

Savage, Rudolph P., Jay Baker, Joseph Golden, Asham Kareem and Billy Manning. 1984. "Hurricane Alicia: Galveston and Houston, Texas, August 17–18, 1983." National Research Council on Natural Disasters, Washington, D.C.: National Academy Press.

Scanlon, T. Jospeh, Jim Jefferson and Debbie Sproat. 1976. "The Port Alice Slide." EPC Field Report 76/1. Ottowa, Ontario: Emergency Planning Canada.

Scheff, Thomas J. 1970. "Towards a Sociological Model of Consensus." In *Social Psychology Through Symbolic Interaction*. Edited by G. P. Stone and H. A. Farberman. Waltham, Massachusetts: Xerox College Publishing.

Selltiz, Claire, Marie Jahoda, Morton Deutsch and Stuart W. Cook. 1959. *Research Methods in Social Relations*. New York: Henry Holt and Co.

Sen, Amartya. 1981. *Poverty and Famine: an Essay on Entitlement and Deprivation*. Oxford: Clarendon Press.

Sharma, Vinod and G. K. Singh. 1985. "Tall Claims, Dubious Practices: Despite Glossy Brochures, UCIL Record is Not All That White." Pp. 81–85 in *Bhopal: Industrial Genocide?* Hong Kong: Arena Press.

Shrivastava, Paul. 1987. *Bhopal: Anatomy of a Crisis*. Cambridge, Mass.: Ballinger.

Simon, Herbert. 1959. "Theories for Decision-Making in Economics and Behavioral Science." *American Economic Review* 49: 253–283.

Simon, Julian L. 1969. *Basic Research Methods in Social Science*. New York: Random House.

Skocpol, Theda. 1979. *States and Social Revolutions*. Cambridge: Cambridge University Press.

Slovic, Paul, Howard Kunreuther and Gilbert F. White. 1974. "Decision Processes, Rationality, and Adjustment to Natural Hazards." In *Natural Hazards: Local, National, and Global*, edited by G. F. White. New York: Oxford University Press.

Sorenson, John H. 1986. Evacuations due to Chemical Accidents: Experience from 1980 to 1984. U.S.D.O.E. Contract No DE-AC05-840R21400. Oak Ridge, Tennessee: Oak Ridge National Laboratory.

Sorenson, J. H. and P. J. Gersmehl. 1980. "Volcanic Hazard Warning System: Persistence and Transferability." *Environmental Management* 4 (March), 125–136.

Starr, Chauncey, 1969. "Social Benefit Versus Technological Risk: What Is Our Society Willing to Pay for Safety?" *Science* 165 (September 19): 1232–1238.

Stinchcombe, Arthur. 1978. *Theoretical Methods in Social History*. New York: Academic Press.

Stone, Philip J., Dexter C. Dunphy, Marshall S. Smith and David M. Ogilvie. 1966. *The General Enquirer: a Computer Approach to Content Analysis*. Cambridge, Mass.: MIT Press.

Super, Susan. 1980. "Pesticides: Worth the Price?" *Agenda* 3(5) June: 17–20.

Sussman, Paul, Phil O'Keefe and Ben Wisner. 1983. "Global Disasters: a Radical Interpretation." In *Interpretations of Calamity*, edited by K. Hewitt. Boston: Allen and Unwin.

Tewari, Madan Mohan. 1982. *External Resources and Economic Development in India*. New Dehli: B. R. Publishing Company.

Thomas, William and Dorothy Swaine Thomas. 1929. *The Child in America*. New York: Alfred A. Knopf.

Times of India. 1985. "Probe Report Gathered Dust for Three Years." 2 January.

Tinker, Jon. 1984. "Are Natural Disasters Natural?" *Socialist Review* 14(6) November–December: 7–25.

Turner, Barry. 1979. "The Social Aetiology of Disasters." *Disasters* 3(1): 53–59.

Twose, Nigel. 1981. *Behind the Weather: Why the Poor Suffer Most; Drought and the Sahel*. OXFAM: Oxford.

U.N. Conference on Trade and Development. 1981. *Handbook of International Trade and Development Statistics*, Supplement (February).

United Nations Environment Programme. 1979. *State of the World Environment, 1979*. Report of the Executive Director of the United Nations Environment Programme. New York: United Nations.

United Nations Yearbook of International Trade Statistics. 1979, Volume 2: Trade by Commodity. New York: United Nations.

U.S. Council on Environmental Quality. 1978. *The Ninth Annual Report of the Council on Environmental Quality*, Washington, D.C.: U.S. Government Printing Office.

U.S. Department of Agriculture. 1979. *The Pesticide Review*. Washington, D.C.: Government Printing Office.

U.S. Nuclear Regulatory Commission. 1984. *Annual Report*. NUREG-1145. Washington, D.C.

Waldbott, George. 1978. *Health Effects of Environmental Pollutants*, 2nd Edition. St. Louis: C. V. Mosby Co.

Wallerstein, Immanuel. 1982. "Crisis as Transition." In *Dynamics of Global Crisis*. New York and London: Monthly Review Press.

———. 1979. "Underdevelopment and Phase B: Effect of Seventeenth Century Stagnation on Core and Periphery of the European World Economy." Pp. 73–83 in *The World System of Capitalism: Past and Present*. Edited by Walter L. Goldfrank. Beverly Hills: Sage Publications.

White, Gilbert F. 1945. "Human Adjustment to Floods." Chicago: University of Chicago Department of Geography, Research Paper 29.

White, Gilbert F. (ed.). 1974. *Natural Hazards: Local, National, Global*. New York: Oxford Unversity Press.

White, Gilbert F. and Gene Haas. 1975. *Assessment of Research on Natural Hazards.* Cambridge, Mass.: MIT Press.

Whorf, Benjamin Lee. 1956. *Language, Thought and Reality.* Cambridge, Mass.: MIT Press.

Wijkman, Anders and Lloyd Timberlake. 1988. *Natural Disasters: Acts of God or Acts of Man?* Philadelphia: New Society Publishers.

INDEX